# VOGUE
# MEN'S KNITS

## Christina Probert

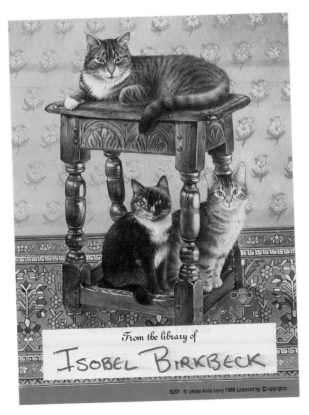

B291 © Lesley Anne Ivory 1989 Licensed by © copyrights

# Acknowledgements

Colour photographs by Perry Ogden 9, 10, 12, 15, 21, 23, 25, 53, 54, 57, 63; Mario Testino 4, 7, 16, 19, 58, 60.

Black and white photographs by Donovan 5; Schall 64; Schatzberg 8; Rand 26.

Details by Steve Kibble; Charts by Andy Ingham.

Hair by Layla D'Angelo 4, 19; Anthony De May for Glemby 7; Nicky Clarke and Ashley Russell both of John Frieda 9, 10, 54, 63; Kerry Warn of New York 21, 23, 25, 53, 57; Orbie 58, 60.

Make-up by Mark Borthwick 4; Jim Brussock 7; Mark Hayles 9, 10, 54, 63; Leslie Chilkes 19; Fran Cooper of New York 21, 23, 25, 53, 57; Kevin 58, 60.

**British Library Cataloguing in Publication Data**

Probert, Christina
  Vogue men's knits. – (Vogue knitting library; 5)
  1. Knitting – Patterns  2. Men's clothing
  I. Title
  646.4'07    TT820

  ISBN 0-948432-35-7

Printed in the Netherlands
by Royal Smeets Offset, Weert
for Angell Editions Limited
Newton Abbot, Devon

# Contents

# Fisherman's Rib Sloppy Joe 1980

*Long, loose fisherman's rib sweater with V-neck, raglan sleeves, ribbed, doubled-over neck border and ribbed welts*

★★　Suitable for adventurous beginners

## MATERIALS

**Yarn**
Sirdar Panorama DK
14(15:16) × 50g. balls

**Needles**
1 pair 3¾mm.
1 pair 4½mm.

## MEASUREMENTS

**Bust**
87(92:97) cm.
34(36:38) in.

**Length**
71(72:73) cm.
27¾(28¼:28½) in.

**Sleeve Seam**
43(44:46) cm.
16¾(17¼:18) in.

## TENSION

21 sts. and 42 rows = 10 cm. (4 in.) square over patt. on 4½mm. needles. If your tension square does not correspond to these measurements, adjust the needle size used.

## ABBREVIATIONS

k.=knit; p.=purl; st(s).=stitch(es); inc.= increas(ing); dec.=decreas(ing); beg.= begin(ning); rem. = remain(ing); rep. = repeat; alt. = alternate; tog. = together; sl. = slip (transfer one stitch from left needle, knitwise unless otherwise stated, to right hand needle.); cont. = continue; patt. = pattern; foll. = following; folls. = follows; mm. = millimetres; cm. = centimetres; in. = inches; st. st. = stocking st.: one row k., one row p.; g. st. = garter st.: every row k.; incs. = increases; decs. = decreases; p.s.s.o. = pass the sl. st. over; t.b.l. = through back of loops; k.1blw. = k. 1 st. below: k. next st. lying 1 row below next st. on left needle, slipping st. off needle in usual way after working.

## BACK

Cast on 101(107:113) sts. with 3¾mm. needles.
Work in rib as folls.:
*1st row:* * k.1, p.1, rep. from * to last st., k.1.
*2nd row:* k.2, * p.1, k.1, rep. from * to last st., k.1.
Work 17 more rows in rib.
Change to 4½mm. needles and work in fisherman's rib as folls.:
*1st row (right side):* k.
*2nd row:* k.1, * p.1, k.1blw., rep. from * to last 2 sts., p.1, k.1.
These 2 rows form fisherman's rib patt.
Cont. in patt. until work measures 46 cm. (18 in.), ending with a 2nd row. **

### Shape Raglan

Dec. 1 st. at each end of next and every foll. 4th row until 67(71:75) sts. rem.
Now dec. 1 st. at each end of every foll. alt. row until 29(31:33) sts. rem.
Work 1 row.
Leave sts. on a spare needle.

## FRONT

Work as for back to **.

### Shape Raglan and Divide for Neck

*Next row:* k.2 tog., k. until there are 49(52:55) sts. on right needle, turn.
Leave rem. sts. on a spare needle.
* Work 3 rows straight.
Dec. 1 st. at raglan edge on next row.
Work 3 rows straight.

### Shape Neck

Cont. dec. 1 st. at raglan edge on next and every foll. 4th row, AT THE SAME TIME dec. 1 st. at neck edge on next and every foll. 8th row until 25(27:28) sts. rem.
Cont. to dec. at neck edge on every 8th row from previous dec. and, AT THE SAME TIME, dec. 1 st. at raglan edge on every alt. row until 2 sts. rem.
Work 1 row.
K.2 tog. and fasten off.
Return to rem. sts., leave centre st. on a thread.
Rejoin yarn, k. to last 2 sts., k.2 tog.
Now work to match other side from *.

## SLEEVES

Cast on 45(45:49) sts. with 3¾mm. needles.
Work 19 rows in rib as for back.
Change to 4½mm. needles.
Work in patt. as for back, inc. 1 st. at each end of 9th and every foll. 10th row until there are 71(73:75) sts.
Cont. without shaping until sleeve measures 43(44:46) cm. (16¾(17¼:18) in.) ending with a 2nd row.

### Shape Raglan

Dec. 1 st. at each end of next and every foll. 4th row until 25(23:21) sts. rem.
Now dec. 1 st. at each end of every foll. alt. row until 11 sts. rem.
Work 1 row.
Leave sts. on safety pin.

## NECKBAND

Sew up raglans, leaving back left raglan seam open.
With right side of work facing and 3¾mm. needles, rib across 11 sts. from left sleeve: k.1, (p.1, k.1) 5 times, pick up and k. 58(62:66) sts. down left side of neck, work centre st. on thread, pick up and k.58(62:66) sts. up right side of neck, work across 11 sts. from sleeve as folls.: (k.1, p.1) 5 times, k.1, then work across sts. from back of neck as folls.: * p.1, k.1, rep. from * to last st., p.1.
*Next row:* rib as set to within 2 sts. of centre st., p.2 tog., p. centre st., p.2 tog. t.b.l., rib to end.
*Next row:* rib to within 2 sts. of centre st., sl.1, k.1, p.s.s.o., k. centre st., k.2 tog., rib to end.
Rep. last 2 rows 3 more times.
Now work 8 rows, inc. 1 st. at each side of centre st. on every alt. row.
Cast off.

## MAKING UP

Sew up raglan and neckband seam.
Fold neckband in half onto inside and catch st. in place.
Sew up side and sleeve seams.

# Fine Sleeveless Pullover

*1933*

*Fine, textured-stitch pullover with round neck, ribbed lower welt, ribbed and shaped neck and armhole borders*

★★ Suitable for knitters with some previous experience

## MATERIALS

### Yarn
Pingouin Pingolaine
4(5:5:6:6) × 50g. balls

### Needles
1 pair 3¼mm.
1 pair 3¾mm.
st. holder

## MEASUREMENTS

### Chest
87(92:97:102:107) cm.
34(36:38:40:42) in.

### Length
57(59:60:62:63) cm.
22¼(23¼:23¾:24¼:24¾) in.

## TENSION

32 sts. and 44 rows = 10 cm. (4 in.) square over patt. on 3¾mm. needles. If your tension square does not correspond to these measurements, adjust the needle size used.

## ABBREVIATIONS

k.=knit; p.=purl; st(s).=stitch(es); inc.= increas(ing); dec.=decreas(ing); beg.= begin(ning); rem. = remain(ing); rep. = repeat; alt. = alternate; tog. = together; sl. = slip (transfer one stitch from left needle, knitwise unless otherwise stated, to right hand needle.); cont. = continue; patt. = pattern; foll. = following; folls. = follows; in. = inches; st. st. = stocking st.: one row k., one row p.; g. st. = garter st.: every row k.; incs. = increases; decs. = decreases; sl. 1p. = sl. 1 st. purlwise.

## FRONT

Cast on 130(138:146:154:162) sts. with 3¼mm. needles.
Work 8 cm. (3¼ in.) in k.2, p.2 rib, inc. 1 st. at beg. of last row. [131(139:147:155: 163) sts.]
Change to 3¾mm. needles and patt. as folls.:
*1st row (right side):* k.1, * sl.1p, k.1, rep. from * to end.
*2nd row:* p.
Rep. these 2 rows to form patt.
Cont. straight in patt. until front measures 15 cm. (5¾ in.), ending with a wrong side row.
Keeping patt. correct, inc. 1 st. at each

end of next and every 6th row until there are 151(159:167:175:183) sts.
Work straight on these sts. until front measures 36(37:38:39:39) cm. (14(14½:15: 15¼:15¼) in.), ending with a wrong side row.

### Shape Armholes
Cast off 5(6:7:8:9) sts. at beg. of next 2 rows.
Cast off 5 sts. at beg. of next 2 rows.
Cast off 2 sts. at beg. of next 4 rows.
Cast off 1 st. at beg. of next 4(4:6:6:8) rows. [119(125:129:135:139) sts.]
Cont. straight until armholes measure (13(14:14:15:16) cm. (5(5½:5½:5¾:6¼) in.), ending with a wrong side row.

### Shape Neck
*1st row:* patt. 51(52:53:54:55), cast off centre 17(21:23:27:29) sts., patt. 51(52:53: 54:55).
Cont. on these sts. for first side, leaving rem. sts. on holder.
Work 1 row.
** Cast off 3 sts. at neck edge on next row.
Dec. 1 st. at neck edge on next and every alt. row, AT THE SAME TIME inc. 1 st. at armhole edge on every 4th row until 35(36:37:38:39) sts. rem., ending at armhole edge.

### Shape Shoulder
Cast off at beg. of next and every alt. row 5 sts. 7(6:5:4:3) times and 6 sts. 0(1:2:3:4) times.
With wrong side of rem. sts. facing, rejoin yarn to neck edge and work as for first side from ** to end.

## BACK

Cast on 114(122:130:138:146) sts. with 3¼mm. needles.
Work in rib as for front, inc. 1 st. at beg. of last row. [115(123:131:139:147) sts.]
Change to 3¾mm. needles.
Work in patt. as for front until work matches front to beg. of inc., ending with a wrong side row.

Inc. 1 st. at each end of next and every 6th row until there are 135(143:151:159:167) sts.
Cont. straight until work matches front to armholes, ending with a wrong side row.

### Shape Armholes
Cast off 4(5:6:7:8) sts. at beg. of next 2 rows.
Cast off 2 sts. at beg. of next 2 rows.
Cast off 1 st. at beg. of next 4(4:6:6:8) rows. [119(125:129:135:139) sts.]
Work straight until armholes measure 17(18:18:19:20) cm. (6½(7:7:7½:7¾) in.), ending with a wrong side row.

### Shape Neck
*1st row:* patt. 34(35:36:37:38), cast off centre 51(55:57:61:63) sts., patt. 34(35:36: 37:38).
Cont. on these sts. for first side leaving rem. sts. on holder.
Dec. 1 st. at neck edge on next and foll. alt.row, AT THE SAME TIME inc. 1 st. at armhole edge on next and foll. 2 alt. rows.

### Shape Shoulder
Work as for front, beg. at armhole edge.
With wrong side of rem. sts. facing, rejoin yarn at neck edge and work as for first side.

## ARMBANDS

Cast on 3 sts. with 3¼mm. needles.
Work in g. st., inc. 1 st. at beg. of every 2nd row until there are 12 sts.
Work straight until band measures 36(37: 38:39:40) cm. (14(14½:15:15¼:15¾) in.) from beg. of straight section.
Dec. 1 st. at shaped edge of next and every alt. row until 3 sts. rem.
Cast off.

## NECKBAND

Cast on 12 sts. with 3¼mm. needles.
Work in g. st. until neckband measures 56(58:61:63:66) cm. (22(22¾:24:24¾:26) in.)
Cast off.

## MAKING UP

Sew up shoulder and side seams.
Sew armbands and neckband into circles by seaming short ends.
Sew long edges of armbands round armholes, overlapping armbands over edge st. of armholes and back-stitching neatly in place.
Sew on neckband round neck as for armbands.
Press lightly under a damp cloth with a warm iron, omitting ribbing and g. st. borders.

# Basketwork-check Waistcoat

1963

*Warm waistcoat in three-colour, stocking-stitch check pattern,*
*with doubled-over, ribbed front and armhole bands, single-rib hem welt*

★★ Suitable for knitters with some previous experience

## MATERIALS

**Yarn**
Pingouin Confort
4(4:5:5:6) × 50g. balls (Main Col. A)
2(2:3:3:3) × 50g. balls (Contrast Col. B)
2(2:3:3:3) × 50g. balls (Contrast Col. C)

**Needles**
1 pair 3mm.
1 pair 4mm.

**Buttons**
5

## MEASUREMENTS

**Chest**
92(97:102:107:112) cm.
36(38:40:42:44) in.

**Length**
57(58:60:61:62) cm.
22¼(22¾:23½:24:24¼) in.

## TENSION

26 sts. and 22 rows = 10 cm. (4 in.) square over patt. on 4mm. needles. If your tension square does not correspond to these measurements, adjust the needle size used.

## ABBREVIATIONS

k.=knit; p.=purl; st(s).=stitch(es); inc.= increase; dec.=decrease; beg.=begin(ning); rem. = remain(ing); rep. = repeat; alt. = alternate; tog. = together; sl. = slip stitch (transfer one stitch from left needle, knitwise unless otherwise stated, to right hand needle.); cont. = continue; patt. = pattern; foll. = following; folls. = follows; mm. = millimetres; cm. = centimetres; in. = inch(es); st.st. = stocking stitch; m.1 = make 1 st.: pick up horizontal loop lying before next st., and work into back of it.

N.B.: When working from chart, carry yarns not in use loosely across wrong side of work to keep fabric elastic. Read odd rows (k. rows) from right to left, and even rows (p. rows) from left to right.

## BACK

Cast on 105(111:117:123:129) sts. with 3mm. needles and A, and work in k.1, p.1 rib, rows on right side having k.1 at each end, for 6 cm. (2¼ in.), ending with a right side row.
*Next row:* rib 2(3:2:2:1), m.1, (rib 4(0:6:6:0), m.1) 5(9:7:13:0) times, (rib 5(5:5:5:6), m.1) 16(21:14:8:21) times, rib to end. [127(133: 139:145:151) sts.]
Change to 4mm. needles.
Work in patt. from chart, rep. the 6 patt. sts. 21(22:23:24:25) times across, working

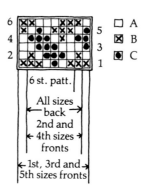

| 6 | ✕✕ | | ✕✕✕ | | |
|---|---|---|---|---|---|
| 4 | ●● | ✕ | ●● | ✕ | |
| 2 | ●● | | ●● | | |
| | ✕✕✕ | | ✕✕ | ✕ | |

□ A
☒ B
◙ C

6 st. patt.
All sizes
← back →
2nd and
← 4th sizes →
fronts
← 1st, 3rd and →
5th sizes fronts

first st. on k. rows and last st. on p. rows as indicated, until back measures 35 cm. (13¾ in.), ending with a wrong side row.

**Shape Armholes**
Cast off 5(5:6:6:7) sts. at beg. of next 2 rows.
Dec. 1 st. at each end of next 5(7:7:9:9) rows.
Work 1 row.
Dec. 1 st. at each end of next and foll. 3(2: 2:1:1) alt. rows. [99(103:107:111:115) sts.]
Work straight until armhole measures 22(23:25:26:27) cm. (8½(9:9¾:10¼:10½) in.), ending with a wrong side row.

**Shape Shoulders**
Cast off 7(7:7:8:8) sts. at beg. of next 6 rows, and 7(8:9:7:8) sts. at beg. of foll. 2 rows.
Cast off rem. 43(45:47:49:51) sts.

## LEFT FRONT

Cast on 53(57:59:63:65) sts. with 3mm. needles and A, and work in rib as for back, ending with a right side row.
*Next row:* rib 4(1:2:4:5), m.1, (rib 5(6:6:6:6), m.1) 9 times, rib to end. [63(67:69:73:75) sts.]
Change to 4mm. needles and work in patt. from chart, rep. the 6 patt. sts. 10(11: 11:12:12) times across, working first 2(1:2: 1:2) sts. and last 1(0:1:0:1) st. on k. rows, and first 1(0:1:0:1) st. and last 2(1:2:1:2) sts. on p. rows as indicated until front matches back to armhole, ending with a wrong side row.

### Shape Armhole and Front Slope
Keeping patt. correct, work as folls.:
*1st row:* cast off 5(5:6:6:7) sts., patt. to last 2 sts., k.2 tog.
*2nd row:* patt.
Dec. 1 st. at armhole edge on next 5(7:7:9:9) rows then on every alt. row 3(2:2:1:1) times, at the same time dec. 1 st. at front slope on next and every foll. alt. row until 43(46:47:50:51) sts. rem.
Cont. dec. 1 st. at front slope *only* on every alt. row until 28(29:30:31:32) sts. rem.
Work straight until armhole matches back to shoulder, ending with a wrong side row.

### Shape Shoulder
Cast off 7(7:7:8:8) sts. at beg. of next and foll. 3 alt. rows.
Work 1 row.
Cast off rem. 7(8:9:7:8) sts.

## RIGHT FRONT

Work as for left front, reversing shapings.

## FRONT BORDERS

Cast on 15 sts. with 3mm. needles and A.
*1st row:* k.7, sl.1, k.7.
*2nd row:* p.
Rep. these 2 rows throughout.
Work straight until border fits up right front from lower edge, around back neck to front slope shaping on left front.
Mark position for 5 buttons on right front, first to come level with front slope, last to come 2 cm. (¾ in.) from lower edge and the others spaced evenly between.
Work 1st buttonhole as folls.:
*Next row:* k.3, cast off 2 sts., k.2 including st. used in casting off, sl.1, k.2, cast off 2 sts., k. to end.
*Next row:* p., casting on 2 sts. over each set cast off.
Work 4 more sets of buttonholes to correspond with button markers.
Complete border.
Cast off.

## ARMHOLE BORDERS

Cast on 11 sts. with 3mm. needles and A.

*1st row:* k.5, sl.1, k.5.
*2nd row:* p.
Rep. these 2 rows until border fits around armhole when slightly stretched.
Cast off.

## MAKING UP

Sew up shoulder and side seams.
Fold front border in half to wrong side and sew in position.
Buttonhole-stitch around double buttonholes.
Join armhole borders into a circle, fold in half to wrong side and sew to armholes.
Press. Sew on buttons.

# Raised Rib-pattern Slipover 1945

*Informal, easy-to-wear slipover in raised-rib pattern, with single rib welts, neck and armhole borders*

★★ Suitable for knitters with some previous experience

## MATERIALS

**Yarn**
Emu Superwash 4 ply
6(6:6:7:7) × 50g. balls

**Needles**
1 pair 2¾mm.
1 pair 3¼mm.

## MEASUREMENTS

**Chest**
92(97:102:107:112) cm.
36(38:40:42:44) in.

**Length**
59(59:60:61:62) cm.
23¼(23¼:23½:24:24½) in.

## TENSION

30 sts. and 38 rows = 10 cm. (4 in.) square over slightly stretched pattern on 3¼mm. needles. If your tension square does not correspond to these measurements, adjust the needle size used.

## ABBREVIATIONS

k.=knit; p.=purl; st(s).=stitch(es); inc.= increase; dec.=decrease; beg.=begin(ning); rem. = remain(ing); rep. = repeat; alt. = alternate; tog. = together; sl. = slip stitch (transfer one stitch from left needle, knit-wise unless otherwise stated, to right hand needle.); cont. = continue; patt. = pattern; foll. = following; folls. = follows; mm. = millimetres; cm. = centimetres; in. = inch(es); st.st. = stocking stitch; p.s.s.o. = pass the slipped stitch over.

## BACK

Cast on 145(151:163:169:175) sts. with 2¾mm. needles.
*1st row:* k.1, * p.1, k.1, rep. from * to end.
*2nd row:* p.1, * k.1, p.1, rep. from * to end.
Rep. these 2 rows until work measures 10 cm. (4 in.), ending with 2nd row and inc. 1 st. on last st. of last row. [146(152:164: 170:176) sts.]
Change to 3¼mm. needles.
Now work in patt.
*1st row:* p.2, * k.1, k. next 2 sts., knitting 2nd st. before 1st st. with the needle taken across front of 1st st., k.1, p.2, rep. from * to end.
*2nd row:* k.2, * p.4, k.2, rep. from * to end.
These 2 rows form the patt.
Cont. in patt. until work measures 34 cm. (13½ in.), ending with 2nd row.

### Shape Armholes

Cast off 7 sts. at beg. of next 2 rows.
Cast off 6 st. at beg. of foll. 2 rows.
Cast off 4 sts. at beg. of foll. 4 rows.
Dec. 1 st. at each end of every alt. row 3 times. [98(104:116:122:128) sts.]
Cont. straight until work measures 23(23:24:25:26) cm. (9(9:9½:9¾:10¼) in.) from beg. of armhole shaping, ending with 2nd row.

### Shape Shoulder

Cast off 7(7:8:9:9) sts. at beg. of next 2 rows.
Cast off 7(8:9:9:10) sts. at beg. of foll. 4 rows.
Cast off 7(7:9:10:10) sts. at beg. of next 2 rows.
Cast off rem. 42(44:46:48:50) sts.

## FRONT

Work as given for back to end of armhole shaping, ending with 2nd row. [98(104:116:122:128) sts.]

### Shape Neckline

*Next row:* patt. 49(52:58:61:64) sts., turn work and leave rem. sts. on spare needle.

Dec. 1 st. at neck edge on next and every foll. 3rd row until 28(30:35:37:39) sts. rem.
Cont. straight in patt. until armhole measures same as back armhole, ending at side edge.

### Shape Shoulder

Cast off 7(7:8:9:9) sts. at beg. of next row.
Work 1 row straight.
Cast off 7(8:9:9:10) sts. at beg. of next and foll. alt. row.
Work 1 row straight.
Cast off rem. 7(7:9:10:10) sts.
With right side of work facing, rejoin yarn to first of rem. 49(52:58:61:64) sts.
Work 1 row straight.
Dec. 1 st. at neck edge of next and every foll. 3rd row until 28(30:35:37:39) sts. rem.
Cont. straight in patt. until armhole measures same as back armhole, ending at side edge.
Shape shoulder as for first front shoulder.

## NECKBAND

Sew up right shoulder seam.
With right side of work facing and 2¾mm. needles, pick up and k. 69(73:75:77:79) sts. down left front neck, 1 st. from centre front, 69(73:75:77:79) sts. up right front neck and 42(44:46:48:50) sts. from back neck. [181(191:197:203:209) sts.].
*1st row:* p.1, * k.1, p.1, rep. from * to 2 sts. before centre st., sl.1, k.1, p.s.s.o., p. centre st., k.2 sts. tog., p.1, ** k.1, p.1, rep. from ** to end.
*2nd row:* * k.1, p.1, rep. from * to 2 sts. before centre st., sl.1, k.1, p.s.s.o., k. centre st., k.2 sts. tog., **p.1, k.1, rep. from ** to end.
Rep. these 2 rows until band measures 3 cm. (1 in.).
Cast off in rib, still dec. at centre.

## SLEEVE BANDS

Sew up left shoulder seam.
With right side of work facing and 2¾mm. needles, pick up 153(153:159:163:169) sts. evenly along armhole.
Work 3 cm. (1 in.) in k.1, p.1, rib, beg. and ending odd-numbered rows with p.1 and even-numbered rows with k.1.
Cast off in rib.

## MAKING UP

Press, very lightly so as not to stretch rib, according to the instructions on the ball bands.
Sew up side seams.

# Snowflake Cardigan

*Raglan-sleeved cardigan in two-colour pattern, with stand-up collar, ribbed welts and garter-stitch front bands*

★★★ Suitable for experienced knitters only

## MATERIALS

**Yarn**
Lister-Lee Motoravia DK
8(9) × 50g. balls (Main Col. A)
8(9) × 50g. balls (Contrast Col. B)

**Needles**
1 pair 3¼mm.
1 pair 4mm.

**Buttons**
10

## MEASUREMENTS

**Chest**
92–97(102–107) cm.
36–38(40–42) in.

## TENSION

22 sts. and 28 rows = 10 cm. (4 in.) square over patt. on 4mm. needles. If your tension square does not correspond to these measurements, adjust the needle size used.

## ABBREVIATIONS

k.=knit; p.=purl; st(s).=stitch(es); inc.= increase; dec.=decrease; beg.=begin(ning); rem. = remain(ing); rep. = repeat; alt. = alternate; tog. = together; sl. = slip stitch (transfer one stitch from left needle, knit-wise unless otherwise stated, to right hand needle.); cont. = continue; patt. = pattern; foll. = following; folls. = follows; mm. = millimetres; cm. = centimetres; in. = inch(es); st.st. = stocking stitch; g.st. = garter st.: every row k.

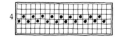

## BACK

Cast on 120(128) sts. with 3¼mm. needles and B.
*1st row:* k.1, * p.1, k.1, rep. from * to end.
*2nd row:* p.1, * k.1, p.1, rep. from * to end.
Rep. these 2 rows for 7 cm. (2¾ in.) ending with 2nd row.
*Next row:* inc. 7 sts. evenly across the row. [127(135) sts.]
Change to 4mm. needles.
Joining in A and breaking off colours as required, cont. in st.st., working in patt. from charts 1, 2, 1, 3, 1, 2, 1.
Cont. repeating patt. in chart 4 as many times as required by raglan.

For right front start at * for all sizes
Rep. from start for back, sleeves and left front

□ A
▣ B

Medium
Large

For back, sleeves and left front start here for

Dec. 1 st. on every row at right edge 24 times.
Dec. 1 st. on alt. rows at right edge 21 times. Cast off on same row as back.

## RIGHT FRONT

Work as for left, reversing design and shapings.

## SLEEVES

Cast on 60(64) sts. with 3¼mm. needles and B.
Work in k.1, p.1 rib for 8 cm. (3¼ in.).
*Next row:* inc. 7(11) sts. evenly across the row. [67(75) sts.]
Change to 4mm. needles.
Work patt. in chart 4, 2(3) times.
Cont. in patt. as for back.
AT THE SAME TIME, inc. 1 st. at the beg. and end of every 5th row. [101(105) sts.]

### Shape Top

Start on same row as back and front shapings.
Dec. 1 st. at beg. and end of next 16(17) rows.
Dec. 1 st. at beg. and end of alt. rows until only 19(21) sts. rem.
Cast off on same row as back and fronts.

## FRONT BANDS

### Right Band

Cast on 9 sts. with 3¼mm. needles and B.
Work in g.st. until band, slightly stretched, fits the front edge of the jacket.
Cast off.

### Left Band

Mark off 10 buttonholes on right band starting at 3 cm. (1 in.) from lower edge and finishing at 1 cm. (½ in.) from top edge.
Work as for right band, incorporating buttonholes as appropriate: k.3, cast off 3, k.3, then cast on 3 sts. on next row.

## COLLAR

Cast on 97(103) sts. with 4mm. needles and B.
Work in st.st. for 6 cm. (2½ in.).
Joining in A as required, work patt. in collar chart.
Break off A.
Work 4 more rows in B.
Cast off.

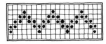

## MAKING UP

Press each piece according to instructions on ball bands. Sew up raglan seams.
Fold collar wrong side out and sew up ends.
Turn collar and backstitch cast-off edge to neckline, keeping right side against right side.
Lift collar and slipstitch cast-on edge to wrong side of neckline.
Sew up front bands.
Sew side and sleeve seams.
Press seams if required. Sew on buttons.

AT THE SAME TIME, when work measures 40(41) cm. (15¾(16) in.), shape raglan.

### Shape Raglan

Dec. 1 st. at beg. and end of next 25 rows.
Dec. 1 st. at beg. and end of alt. rows until 37(41) sts. rem.
Cast off.

## LEFT FRONT

Cast on 60(64) sts. with 3¼mm. needles and B.
Work in k.1, p.1 rib for 7 cm. (2¾ in.) ending with 2nd row.
*Next row:* inc. 6 sts. evenly across the row. [66(70) sts.]
Change to 4mm. needles.
Work charts as for back until work measures 40(41) cm. (15¾(16) in.).

### Shape Raglan

Start on same row as back shaping.

# Chunky, Ribbed, Country Sweater 1968

*Soft, roomy sweater with saddle shoulders, in textured rib pattern, with single-rib lower edge, cuff and hemmed neck welts*

★★ Suitable for knitters with some previous experience

## MATERIALS

**Yarn**
Hunter Embo 3 ply (Heavyweight yarn) 11(12:13:13:14) × 112g. hanks

**Needles**
1 pair 5mm.
1 pair 6mm.

## MEASUREMENTS

**Chest**
92(97:102:107:112) cm.
36(38:40:42:44) in.

**Length**
66(67:69:70:71) cm.
26(26¼:27¼:27½:28) in.

**Sleeve Seam**
46(46:47:47:48) cm.
18(18:18½:18½:19) in.

## TENSION

18 sts. and 20 rows = 10 cm. (4 in.) square over patt. on 6mm. needles. If your tension square does not correspond to these measurements, adjust the needle size used.

## ABBREVIATIONS

k.=knit; p.=purl; st(s).=stitch(es); inc.= increase; dec.=decrease; beg.=begin(ning);

rem. = remain(ing); rep. = repeat; alt. = alternate; tog. = together; sl. = slip stitch (transfer one stitch from left needle, knit-wise unless otherwise stated, to right hand needle.); cont. = continue; patt. = pattern; foll. = following; folls. = follows; mm. = millimetres; cm. = centimetres; in. = inch(es); st.st. = stocking stitch; m.1 = make 1 st.: pick up horizontal loop lying before next st. and work into back of it; tw.2 = twist 2: k. into back of 2nd st., then front of first st. on left-hand needle and sl. 2 sts. off needle tog.

## BACK

** Cast on 80(86:90:96:100) sts. with 5mm. needles and work in k.1, p.1 rib for 8 cm. (3¼ in.).
*Next row:* rib 5(2:5:3:5), m.1, rib 7(9:8:10:9), m.1 10(9:10:9:10) times, rib to end. [91(96:101:106:111) sts.]
Change to 6mm. needles and work in patt. as folls.:
*1st row:* (right side): k.2, * tw.2, k.1, p.1, k.1, rep. from * to last 4 sts., tw.2, k.2.
*2nd row:* k.2, * p.2, k.3, rep. from * to last 4 sts., p.2, k.2.
These 2 rows form patt.
Cont. in patt. until back measures 44 cm. (17¼ in.), ending with a wrong side row.

**Shape Armholes**
Cast off 6(6:6:7:7) sts. at beg. of next 2 rows.
Dec. 1 st. at each end of next and every row 69(72:75:78:81) sts. rem.
Work straight until armholes measure 17(18:20:21:22) cm. (6½(7:7¾:8¼:8½) in.), ending with a wrong side row. **

**Shape Shoulders**
Cast off 4 sts. at beg. of next 10(8:8:6:4) rows, then 5 sts. at beg. of foll. 0(2:2:4:6) rows.
Cast off rem. 29(30:33:34:35) sts.

## FRONT

Work as for back from ** to **.

**Shape Shoulders and Front Neck**
*Next row:* patt. 27(28:28:29:30), cast off 15(16:19:20:21) sts., patt. to end.
Cont. on these sts. for first side.
*1st row:* cast off 4 sts., patt. to last 2 sts., k.2 tog.
*2nd row:* k.2 tog., patt. to end.
Rep. last 2 rows once more.
*Next row:* cast off 4(4:4:4:5) sts., patt. to last 2 sts., k.2 tog.
*Next row:* k.2 tog., patt. to end.

*Next row:* cast off 4(4:4:5:5) sts., patt. to last 2 sts., k.2 tog.
*Next row:* patt.
Cast off rem. 4(5:5:5:5) sts.
With wrong side facing, rejoin yarn to rem. sts. and work to match first side, reversing shapings.

## SLEEVES

Cast on 38(38:40:40:42) sts. with 5mm. needles and work in k.1, p.1 rib for 8 cm. (3¼ in.).
*Next row:* rib 8(8:2:2:1), m.1, rib 11(11:7:7:5), m.1 2(2:5:5:8) times, rib to end. [41(41:46:46:51) sts.]
Change to 6mm. needles and, working in patt. as given for back, shape sides by inc. 1 st. at each end of 3rd and every foll. 4th row until there are 71(71:76:76:81) sts., taking inc. sts. into patt.
Work straight until sleeve seam measures 46(46:47:47:48) cm. (18(18:18½:18½:18¾) in.), ending with a wrong side row.

**Shape Top**
Cast off 6(6:6:7:7) sts. at beg. of next 2 rows.
Dec. 1 st. at each end of next and every foll. alt. row until 37(33:34:26:31) sts. rem.
Work 1 row.
Dec. 1 st. at each end of every row until 17(17:18:18:19) sts. rem.
Work 22(24:24:24:26) rows on these sts. for saddle shoulder.
Cast off.

## MAKING UP AND NECK BORDER

Sew saddles to shoulders, leaving left back shoulder open.

**Neck Border**
With right side facing and 5mm. needles, k. up 15(15:16:16:17) sts. from left saddle shoulder, 9 sts. down left side of neck, 15(16:19:20:21) sts. from the front, 9 sts. up right side of neck, 15(15:16:16:17), sts. from right saddle shoulder, 27(28:31: 32:33) sts. from back. [90(92:100:102: 106) sts.]
Work in k.1, p.1 rib for 15 cm. (6 in.).
With a 6mm. needle, cast off loosely in rib.
Sew up left back saddle seam and neck border.
Fold neck border in half to wrong side and slip-hem in position.
Sew up side and sleeve seams.
Set in sleeves.
Press seams.

# Broken Cable Heavyweight Sweater

*Hip-length sweater in broken cable pattern with ribbed welts*

★★ Suitable for knitters with some previous experience

## MATERIALS

**Yarn**
Sirdar Countrystyle DK
14(14:15) × 50g balls

**Needles**
1 pair 3¼mm.
1 pair 4mm.
1 cable needle
st. holders

## MEASUREMENTS

**Chest**
97(102:107) cm.
38(40:42) in.

**Length**
66(68:70) cm.
26(26¾:27½) in.

**Sleeve Seam**
46(49:50) cm.
18(19¼:19½) in.

## TENSION

30 sts. and 30 rows = 10 cm. (4 in.) square over patt. on 4mm. needles. If your tension square does not correspond to these measurements, adjust the needle size used.

## ABBREVIATIONS

k.=knit; p.=purl; st(s).=stitch(es); inc.= increas(ing); dec.=decreas(ing); beg.= begin(ning); rem. = remain(ing); rep. = repeat; alt. = alternate; tog. = together; sl. = slip (transfer one stitch from left needle, knitwise unless otherwise stated, to right hand needle.); cont. = continue; patt. = pattern; foll. = following; folls. = follows; inc. = increases; decs. = decreases; CR2R = sl. next 2 sts. on cable needle and leave at back, k.2, then p.2 from cable needle; CR2L = sl. next 2 sts. on cable needle and leave at front, p.2, then k.2 from cable needle; m.1 = make 1 st.: pick up horizontal loop lying before next st. and k. into the back of it.

## BACK

Cast on 120(124:128) sts. with 3¼mm. needles.
Work in k.2, p.2 rib for 8(10:12) cm. (3¼(4:4¾) in.), ending with a wrong side row.
*Next row:* rib 2(2:1) m.1, (rib 3, m.1) 39(40:42) times, rib to end. [160(165:161) sts.]

1st size: p. next row. [160 sts.]
2nd size: p. next row, inc. 3 sts. evenly across row. [168 sts.]
3rd size: p. next row, inc. 3 sts. evenly across row. [174 sts.]
All sizes:
Change to 4mm. needles.
Work in patt. as folls.:
*1st row (right side):* p.7(4:7), k.6, (p.8, k.6) 10(11:11) times, p.7(4:7).
*2nd row:* k.7(4:7), p.6, (k.8, p.6) 10(11:11) times, k.7(4:7).
*3rd row:* as 1st.
*4th row:* as 2nd.
*5th row:* p.5(2:5), * CR2R, k.2, CR2L, p.4, rep. from * to end, ending last rep. p.5(2:5).
*6th row:* k.5(2:5), * (p.2, k.2) twice, p.2, k.4, rep. from * to end, ending last rep. k.5(2:5).
*7th row:* p.5(2:5), * (k.2, p.2) twice, k.2, p.4, rep. from * to end, ending last rep. p.(5:2:5).
*8th, 10th, 12th, 14th, 16th, 18th rows:* as 6th.
*9th, 11th, 13th, 15th, 17th rows:* as 7th.
*19th row:* p.5(2:5), * CR2L., k.2, CR2R, p.4, rep. from * to end, ending last rep. p.5(2:5).
*20th row:* as 2nd.
*21st row:* as 1st.
*22nd row:* as 2nd.
These 22 rows form patt.
Cont. straight in patt. until back measures 43(44:45) cm. (16¾(17¼:17¾) in.), ending with a wrong side row.

### Shape Armholes

Cast off 13(10:13) sts. at beg. of next 2 rows. [134(148:148) sts.] **
Cont. on rem. sts. in patt. as set, until armholes measure 23(24:25) cm. (9(9½:9¾) in.) from cast-off edge of arm-shaping, ending with a wrong side row.

### Shape Shoulders

Cast off 44(51:51) sts. at beg. of next 2 rows.
Leave rem. sts. on a holder.

## FRONT

Work as for back to **
Cont. on rem. sts. in patt. until armholes measure 17(18:19) cm. (6½(7:7½) in.), ending with a wrong side row.

### Shape Neck

*Next row:* patt. 54(61:61) sts., turn, work on these sts. only.
Sl. rem. sts. onto spare needle.
Dec. 1 st. at neck edge on next 6 rows, then on every foll. alt. row until 44(51:51) sts. rem.
Work a few rows straight on rem. sts. until same number of rows have been worked as for back to shoulder line,

ending with a wrong side row.

### Shape Shoulder

Cast off all sts. in patt.
Sl. centre 26 sts. onto holder.
Rejoin yarn to inner end of rem. 54(61:61) sts. and complete to match first side.

## SLEEVES

Cast on 60(64:68) sts. with 3¼mm. needles.
Work in k.2, p.2, rib for 8(10:12) cm. (3¼(4:4¾) in.), ending with a wrong side row.
*Next row (right side):* rib 4(6:8), m.1, (rib 1, m.1) 51(51:53) times, rib to end. [112(116:122) sts.]
*1st and 2nd sizes:* p. next row.
*3rd size:* p. next row, inc. 1 st. at each end of this row. [112(116:124) sts.]
Change to 4mm. needles and cont. in patt. as folls.:
*1st row (right side):* p.4(6:3), k.6 (p.8, k.6) 7(7:8) times, p.4(6:3).
*2nd row (wrong side):* k.4(6:3), p.6, (k.8, p.6) 7(7:8) times, k.4(6:3).
Cont. on sts. as set, working in patt. as for back.
Inc. 1 st. at each end of every 8th row until there are 140(144:150) sts., working extra sts. into patt.
Work on all sts. in patt. until sleeve measures 50(52:54) cm. (19½(20½:21¼) in.) from cast-on edge, ending with a wrong side row.
*Next row:* cast off all sts. in patt.

## NECKBAND

Sew up right shoulder seam.
With 3¼mm. needles and right side facing, pick up and k. foll. sts., 20 sts. from left side front, 26 sts. from centre front, 20 sts. from right side front and 46 sts. from centre back. [112 sts.]
Work 3 cm. (1¼ in.) in k.2, p.2 rib.
Cast off ribwise.

## MAKING UP

Sew up rem. shoulder seam and neck-band seam.
Set in sleeves, sewing last 13(10:13) row-ends of sleeves to cast-off sts. of back and front armhole shaping.
Sew up side and sleeve seams.

# Giant Cable-stitch Sweater

*Warm sweater with cable bands on moss stitch, set-in sleeves, ribbed turtle neck and welts*

★★ Suitable for knitters with some previous experience

## MATERIALS

### Yarn
Sirdar Countrystyle DK
13(13:14:14) × 50g. balls

### Needles
1 pair 3¼mm.
1 pair 4mm.
1 cable needle
st. holder

## MEASUREMENTS

### Chest
97(102:107:112) cm.
38(40:42:44) in.

### Length
62(64:66:68) cm.
24¼(25:26:26¾) in.

### Sleeve Seam
47(48:49:50) cm.
18½(18¾:19¼:19½) in.

## TENSION

23 sts. and 34 rows = 10 cm. (4 in.) square over m.st. on 4mm. needles. If your tension square does not correspond to these measurements, adjust the needle size used.

## ABBREVIATIONS

k. = knit; p. = purl; st(s). = stitch(es); inc. = increas(ing); dec. = decreas(ing); beg. = begin(ning); rem. = remain(ing); rep. = repeat; alt. = alternate; tog. = together; sl. = slip (transfer one stitch from left needle, knitwise unless otherwise stated, to right hand needle.); cont. = continue; patt. = pattern; foll. = following; folls. = follows; mm. = millimetres; cm. = centimetres; in. = inches; st. st. = stocking st.: one row k., one row p.; g. st. = garter st.: every row k.; incs. = increases; decs. = decreases; m.1 = make 1 st.: pick up horizontal loop lying before next st. and

k. into the back of it; C6B = cable 6 back: sl. next 6 sts. onto cable needle and leave at back, k. 6 sts., then k.6 from cable needle.

## BACK

Cast on 112(116:120:124) sts. with 3¼mm. needles.
Work 8(9:10:11) cm. (3¼(3½:4:4¼) in.) in k.2, p.2 rib, ending with a right side row.
*Next row:* rib 9(1:3:5), m.1, (rib 5(6:5:5), m.1) 19(19:23:23) times, rib to end. [132(136:144:148) sts.]
Change to 4mm. needles and work in patt. as folls.:
*1st row (right side):* m. st. 25(25:27:27), (k.12, m. st. 23(25:27:29)) twice, k.12, m. st. 25(25:27:27).
*2nd row:* m. st. 25(25:27:27), (p.12, m. st. 23(25:27:29)) twice, p.12, m. st. 25(25:27:27).
Rep. 1st and 2nd rows three more times.
*9th row:* m. st. 25(25:27:27), (C6B, m. st. 23(25:27:29)) twice, C6B, m. st. 25(25:27:27).
*10th row:* as 2nd.
*11th, 13th and 15th rows:* as 1st.
*12th, 14th and 16th rows:* as 2nd.
These 16 rows form the patt. and are repeated throughout.
Cont. straight in patt. until back measures 42(43:44:45) cm. (16½(16¾:17¼:17¾) in.) from cast-on edge, ending with a wrong side row.

### Shape Armholes
Cast off 5 sts. at beg. of next 2 rows.
Dec. 1 st. at each end of next and every foll. alt. row until 110(114:122:126) sts. rem. **
Cont. straight in patt. on rem. sts. until armholes measure 20(21:22:23) cm. (7¾(8¼:8½:9) in.) from beg. of armhole shaping, ending with a wrong side row.

### Shape Shoulders
Cast off 36(37:40:41) sts. at beg. of next 2 rows, in patt.
Leave rem. 38(40:42:44) sts. on holder.

## FRONT

Work as for back to **.
Cont. straight in patt. on rem. sts. until armholes measure 13(14:14:15) cm. (5(5½:5½:5¾) in.) from beg. of armhole shaping, ending with a wrong side row.

### Shape Neck
*Next row:* patt. 46(47:50:51) sts., cast off centre 18(20:22:24) sts., patt. to end.
Now work on last group of sts. only, sl. rem. sts. onto spare needle.
Dec. 1 st. at neck edge on next and every

foll. alt. row 10 times in all. [36(37:40:41) sts.]
Cont. straight on rem. sts. until armhole measures 20(21:22:23) cm. (7¾(8¼:8½:9) in.) from beg. of armhole shaping, ending with a right side row.

### Shape Shoulder
Cast off in patt.
Return to sts. on spare needle, rejoin yarn and complete left side of neck as for right side, reversing shapings.

## SLEEVES

Cast on 56(56:60:60) sts. with 3¼mm. needles.
Work 8(9:10:11) cm. (3¼(3½:4:4¼) in.), in k.2, p.2 rib, ending with a right side row.
*Next row:* rib 8(8:12:12), m.1, (rib 2, m.1) 20(20:18:18) times, rib to end. [77(77:79:79) sts.]
Change to 4mm. needles and work in patt. as folls.:
*1st row (right side):* m. st. 15, k.12, m. st. 23(23:25:25). k.12, m. st. 15.
*2nd row:* m. st. 15, p.12, m. st. 23(23:25:25), p.12, m. st. 15.
Cont. on sts. as set, foll. patt. as given for back.
Inc. 1 st. at each end of 15th and every foll. 16th row until there are 93(93:95:95) sts. on needle, working extra sts. into m. st. patt.
Cont. straight on all sts. until sleeve measures 47(48:49:50) cm. (18½(18¾:19¼:19½) in.) from cast-on edge, ending with a wrong side row.

### Shape Top
Cast off 5 sts. at beg. of next 2 rows.
Dec. 1 st. at each end of every foll. alt. row until 41 sts. rem.
Cast off 3 sts. at beg. of next 6(6:8:8) rows.
Cast off rem. sts.

## POLO COLLAR

Sew up right shoulder seam.
With 4mm. needles, pick up and k. 32(32:34:34) sts. from left side front, 18(20:22:24) sts. from centre front, 32(32:34:34) sts. from right side front and 38(40:42:44) sts. from centre back. [120(124:132:136) sts.]
Work 15 cm. (5¾ in.) in k.2, p.2 rib.
Cast off in rib.

## MAKING UP

Do not press.
Sew up rem. shoulder seam and polo collar seam.
Sew up side and sleeve seams.
Set in sleeves.

# Finely Cabled Sweater

### Lightweight, round-necked sweater with allover fine cable pattern, ribbed welts and hemmed neck border

★★ Suitable for knitters with some previous experience

## MATERIALS

**Yarn**
Rowan Botany 3 ply
9(9:10:10) × 50g. balls

**Needles**
1 pair 2¼mm.
1 pair 3mm.
1 cable needle

## MEASUREMENTS

**Chest**
92(97:102:107) cm.
36(38:40:42) in.

**Length**
64(65:67:68) cm.
25(25½:26¼:26¾) in.

**Sleeve Seam**
46(46:47:47) cm.
18(18:18½:18½) in.

## TENSION

40 sts. and 48 rows = 10 cm. (4 in.) square over patt. on 3mm. needles. If your tension square does not correspond to these measurements, adjust the needle size used.

## ABBREVIATIONS

k.=knit; p.=purl; st(s).=stitch(es); inc.= increase; dec.=decrease; beg.=begin(ning);

rem. = remain(ing); rep. = repeat; alt. = alternate; tog. = together; sl. = slip stitch (transfer one stitch from left needle, knitwise unless otherwise stated, to right hand needle.); cont. = continue; patt. = pattern; foll. = following; folls. = follows; mm. = millimetres; cm. = centimetres; in. = inch(es); st.st. = stocking stitch; m.1 = make 1 st. by picking up horizontal loop lying before next st. and working into back of it; C6B = cable 6 back: slip next 3 sts. onto cable needle and leave at back of work, k.3, then k.3 from cable needle.

## BACK

** Cast on 146(154:164:172) sts. with 2¼mm. needles and work in k.1, p.1 rib for 8 cm. (3¼ in.).
*Next row:* rib 5(8:14:17), m.1, (rib 3, m.1) 45(46:45:46) times, rib to end. [192(201: 210:219) sts.]
Change to 3mm. needles and work in patt. as folls.:
*1st and 3rd rows:* p.1, k.1, p.1, * k.6, p.1, k.1, p.1, rep. from * to end.
*2nd and 4th rows:* k.3, * p.6, k.3, rep. from * to end.
*5th row:* p.1, k.1, p.1, * C6B, p.1, k.1, p.1, rep. from * to end.
*6th row:* as 2nd.
*7th row:* as 1st.
*8th row:* as 2nd.
These 8 rows form patt.
Work in patt. until back measures 42 cm. (16½ in.), ending with right side facing.

### Shape Armholes

Cast off 7(8:9:10) sts. at beg. of next 2 rows.
Dec. 1 st. at each end of next and every foll. alt. row until 154(159:160:165) sts. rem. **
Work straight until armholes measure 22(23:25:26) cm. (8½(9:9¾:10¼) in.) ending with right side facing.

### Shape Shoulders

Cast off 9 sts. at beg. of next 8 rows, then 9(9:9:10) sts. at beg. of foll. 2 rows. Leave rem. 64(69:70:73) sts. on a spare needle.

## FRONT

Work as for back from ** to **.
Work straight until armholes measure 15(16:18:18) cm. (5¾(6¼:7:7) in.), ending with right side facing.

### Shape Front Neck

*Next row:* patt. 59(61:61:63) sts., k.2 tog., turn and leave rem. sts. on a spare needle.

Cont. on these sts. for first side, dec. 1 st. at neck edge on every row until 45(45: 45:46) sts. rem.
Work straight until armhole matches back to shoulder, ending with right side facing.

### Shape Shoulder

Cast off 9 sts. at beg. of next and foll. 3 alt. rows. Work 1 row.
Cast off rem. 9(9:9:10) sts.
With right side facing, slip centre 32(33: 34:35) sts. onto a length of yarn, rejoin yarn to neck edge of rem. sts., k.2 tog., patt. to end.
Work to match first side, reversing shapings.

## SLEEVES

Cast on 78(82:86:90) sts. with 2¼mm. needles and work in k.1, p.1, rib for 9 cm. (3½ in.).
*Next row:* rib 4(3:7:5), m.1, (rib 3(4:3:4), m.1) 23(19:24:20) times, rib to end. [102(102:111:111) sts.]
Change to 3mm. needles and work in patt. as given for back, *shaping sides* by inc. 1 st. at each end of 5th and every foll. 6th row until there are 156(156:165:165) sts. taking inc. sts. into patt.
Work straight until sleeve measures 46(46: 47:47) cm. (18(18:18½:18½) in.), ending with same row of patt. as on back and front.

### Shape Top

Cast off 7(8:9:10) sts. at beg. of next 2 rows.
Dec. 1 st. at each end of next and every alt. row until 84(72:69:53) sts. rem.
Work 1 row.
Dec. 1 st. at each end of every row until 40(40:41:41) sts. rem.
Cast off rem. sts.

## MAKING UP AND NECK BORDER

Sew up right shoulder seam.
With right side facing, using 2¼mm. needles, k. up 28(28:28:32) sts. down left side of neck, k.32(33:34:35) sts. from front, k. up 28(28:28:32) sts. up right side of neck, k.64(69:70:73) sts. from back. [152(158:160:172) sts.]
Work in k.1, p.1, rib for 7 cm. (2¾ in.).
Using a 3mm. needle, cast off loosely in rib.
Sew up left shoulder and neck border.
Fold neck border in half to wrong side and slip-hem loosely in position.
Sew up side and sleeve seams.
Sew in sleeves.

# Wave-stitch, V-neck Sweater

1940

*Decorative, yet very simple, unisex V-neck sweater in wave stitch, with set-in sleeves and firmly ribbed welts*

★★ Suitable for knitters with some previous experience

## MATERIALS

**Yarn**
Patons Clansman 4 ply
9(9:10:10:11:11) × 50g. balls

**Needles**
1 pair 2¾mm.
1 pair 3¼mm.

## MEASUREMENTS

**Bust/Chest**
82(87:92:97:102:107) cm.
32(34:36:38:40:42) in.

**Length**
61(62:63:65:66:67) cm.
24(24¼:24¾:25½:26:26¼) in.

**Sleeve Seam**
42(43:44:46:47:47) cm.
16½(16¾:17¼:18:18½:18½) in.

## TENSION

28 sts. and 40 rows = 10 cm. (4 in.) square over patt. on 3¼mm. needles. If your tension square does not correspond to these measurements, adjust the needle size used.

## ABBREVIATIONS

k.=knit; p.=purl; st(s).=stitch(es); inc.= increase; dec.=decrease; beg.=begin(ning); rem. = remain(ing); rep. = repeat; alt. = alternate; tog. = together; sl. = slip stitch (transfer one stitch from left needle, knitwise unless otherwise stated, to right hand needle.); cont. = continue; patt. = pattern; foll. = following; folls. = follows; mm. = millimetres; cm. = centimetres; in. = inch(es); st.st. = stocking stitch.

## BACK

Cast on 105(113:121:129:137:145) sts. with 2¾mm. needles.
*1st row:* k.2, * p.1, k.1, rep. from * to last st., k.1.
*2nd row:* k.1, * p.1, k.1, rep. from * to end.
These 2 rows form rib.
Cont. until work measures 7 cm. (2¾ in.), dec. 3 sts. during last row. [102(110:118: 126:134:142) sts.]
Change to 3¼mm. needles.
*1st row:* k.
*2nd row:* p.
*3rd row:* k.
*4th row:* k.6, * p.2, k.6, rep. from * to end.
*5th row:* p.6, * k.2, p.6, rep. from * to end.
*6th and 7th rows:* as 4th and 5th.
*8th row:* as 4th.
*9th row:* k.

*10th row:* p.
*11th row:* k.
*12th row:* k.2, * p.2, k.6, rep. from * to last 4 sts., p.2, k.2.
*13th row:* p.2, * k.2, p.6, rep. from * to last 4 sts., k.2, p.2.
*14th and 15th rows:* as 12th and 13th.
*16th row:* as 12th.
These 16 rows form the patt.
Cont. in patt. and shape sides by inc. 1 st. at each end of next row, then on every foll. 14th row until there are 118(126:134:142: 150:158) sts., incorporating extra sts. into patt.
Cont. straight until work measures 43 cm. (16¾ in.), not stretched, ending after a row worked on wrong side.

### Shape Armholes

Cast off 5(6:7:8:9:10) sts. at beg. of next 2 rows. **
Dec. 1 st. at each end of next 3(3:5:5:5:5) rows, then on every alt. row until 96(100:106:110:116:120) sts. rem.
Cont. without shaping until work measures 61(62:63:65:66:67) cm., 24(24¼: 24¾:25½:26:26¼) in. at centre, not stretched, ending after a row worked on wrong side.

### Shape Shoulders

Cast off 10(10:11:11:12:12) sts. at beg. of next 4 rows, then 10(11:11:12:12:13) sts. at beg. of next 2 rows.
Cast off rem. sts.

## FRONT

Work as for back to **
Dec. 1 st. at each end of next 2(2:4:4:4:4) rows.

### Shape Neck

*Next row:* work 2 tog., patt. 50(53:54:57: 60:63), turn.
Cont. on this group.
Dec. 1 st. at both edges on every right-side row until 45(46:51:52:55:56) sts. rem.
Cont. dec. at neck edge only on every right-side row until 40(42:45:47:50:52) sts. rem., then on every foll. 4th row until 30(31:33:34:36:37) sts. rem.
Cont. straight until front measures same as back to shoulder shaping, ending at armhole edge.

**Shape Shoulder**

Cast off 10(10:11:11:12:12) sts. at beg. of next and foll. alt. row.
Work 1 row. Cast off.
Rejoin yarn to sts. left for other side and work to match first side, reversing all shapings.

## SLEEVES

Cast on 55(57:59:61:63:65) sts. with 2¾mm. needles and work 7 cm. (2¾ in.) in rib as on back, ending after a 1st row.
*Next row:* rib 3(4:4:2:10:2), * inc. in next st., rib 7(11:4:6:2:4), rep. from * to last 4(5:5:3:11:3) sts., inc. in next st., rib to end. [62(62:70:70:78:78) sts.]
Change to 3¼mm. needles and patt. as on front, inc. 1 st. at each end of 17th row, then on every foll. 6th row until there are 74(92:88:106:102:118) sts., then on every foll. 8th row until there are 92(98:104:110:116:122) sts., incorporating extra sts. into patt.
Cont. straight until work measures approx. 42(43:44:46:47:47) cm., 16½(16¾:

17¼:18:18½:18½) in., ending after similar patt. row as on back before armhole shaping.

**Shape Sleeve Top**

Cast off 5(6:7:8:9:10) sts. at beg. of next 2 rows.
Work 4 rows straight.
Dec. 1 st. at each end of every right-side row until 44 sts. rem., then on every row until 30 sts. rem.
Cast off.

## NECKBAND

Sew up shoulder seams.
Cast on 2 sts. with 2¾mm. needles.
*1st row:* p.2.
*2nd row:* (k.1, p.1) into first st., then (p.1, k.1) into next st.
*3rd row:* p.1, k.2, p.1.
*4th row:* k.1, (p.1, k.1) into next st., (k.1, p.1) into next st., k.1.
*5th row:* p.1, k.1, p.2, k.1, p.1.
*6th row:* k.1, p.1, (k.1, p.1) into next st., (p.1, k.1) into next st., p.1, k.1.

Cont. in this way working 2 into each of the 2 centre sts. of every even row, and working all sts. into rib, until there are 24 sts.
*Next row:* rib.
*Next row:* rib 12, turn and leave rem. sts. on a spare needle.
Cont. on these 12 sts. until strip fits up front edge and round to centre back of neck, allowing for rib to be a little stretched.
Cast off in rib.
Rejoin yarn to centre edge of rem. sts. and work 2nd strip as first.

## MAKING UP

Omitting welt and cuffs, press lightly using a warm iron and damp cloth.
Sew up side and sleeve seams.
Set in sleeves.
Sew neckband in position, slightly overlapping edge of neckband over main part and joining ends at back of neck.
Press seams.

---

# Moroccan, Multicoloured Waistcoat

*Sleeveless waistcoat in ten-colour allover pattern incorporating Moroccan motifs, with front and armhole borders in striped rib*

★★★ Suitable for experienced knitters only

## MATERIALS

**Yarn**
Natural Dye Company Wool
Naturally dyed woollen yarn sold as pack including 5 handmade Dorset buttons (not photographed). Pack contains 75g. in col. A, 50g. each in cols. F and M, 25g. each in cols. B, C, D, E, G, H, J. Cols. vary according to dye ingredients: here A = grey, B = white, C = gold, D = biscuit, E = salmon pink, F = purple, G = rust, H = mauve, M = marled green, J = wine.

**Needles**
1 pair 2¼mm.
1 pair 3mm.

**Buttons**
included in pack: 5

## MEASUREMENTS

**Chest**
92(97:102:107:112) cm.
36(38:40:42:44) in.

**Length**
62(63:65:66:67) cm.
24¼(24¾:25½:26:26¼ in.)

## TENSION

20 sts. = 7 cm. (2¾ in.) over st.st. on 3mm. needles. If your tension does not correspond to these measurements, adjust the needle size used.

## ABBREVIATIONS

k.=knit; p.=purl; st(s).=stitch(es); inc.= increase; dec.=decrease; beg.=begin(ning); rem. = remain(ing); rep. = repeat; alt. = alternate; tog. = together; sl. = slip stitch (transfer one stitch from left needle, knitwise unless otherwise stated, to right hand needle.); cont. = continue; patt. = pattern; foll. = following; folls. = follows; mm. = millimetres; cm. = centimetres; in. = inch(es); st.st. = stocking stitch.

## BACK

Beg. striped patt.
Cast on 127(135:143:151:159) sts., with

3mm. needles and H.
*1st row:* with H, k. to end.
*2nd row:* with A, p. to end.
*3rd row:* with A, k. to end.
*4th row:* as 2nd.
*5th row:* as 3rd.
*6th row:* with F, p. to end.
*7th row:* with G, k. to end.
*8th row:* with D, p. to end.
*9th row:* with M, k. to end.
*10th row:* with M, p. to end.
*11th row:* as 9th.
*12th row:* as 10th.
*13th row:* with J, k. to end.
*14th row:* with D, p. to end.
These 14 rows form patt.
Cont. in patt. until work measures 39 cm. (15¼ in.) from beg., ending with a p. row.

**Shape Armholes**
Keeping patt. correct, cast off at beg. of next and every row 5 sts. twice and 4 sts. twice.
Dec. 1 st. at each end of next and every alt. row until 97(103:109:115:121) sts. rem.
Cont. without shaping until armholes measure 23(24:26:27:28) cm. (9(9½:10¼:

10½:11) in.) from beg., ending with a p. row.

**Shape Shoulders**

Cast off at beg. of next and every row 7(8:8:9:9) sts. 6 times and 7(6:8:7:9) sts. twice.

Cast off rem. 41(43:45:47:49) sts.

## LEFT FRONT

Cast on 68(72:76:80:84) sts. with 3mm. needles and G. Begin patt.

N.B. ALL ODD ROWS ARE K., ALL EVEN ROWS ARE P.:

*1st row:* G.
*2nd row:* B.
*3rd row:* C.
*4th row:* B.
*5th row:* D.
*6th row:* * 3E, 2G, rep. from * to last 3(2:1:0:4) sts., 3(2:1:0:4)E.
*7th row:* (2E, 2G(1E, 2G:2G:1G:0)), * 3E, 2G, rep. from * to last 4 sts., 3E, 1G.
*8th row:* F.
*9th row:* G.
*10th row:* H.
*11th row:* (1B, 3M, 6E(2E:6E:1B, 3M, 6E:2E)), *1B, 4M, 1B, 6E, rep. from * to last 10 sts., 1B, 4M, 1B, 4E.
*12th row:* 3E, * 1B, 6M, 1B, 4E, rep. from * to last 5(9:1:5:9) sts., 1B, 4M(1B, 6M, 1B, 1E:1B:1B, 4M:1B, 6M, 1B, 1E).
*13th row:* (3B, 2M, 1B, 2E(0:1M, 1B, 2E:3B, 2M, 1B, 2E:0)), * 1B, 2M, 4B, 2M, 1B, 2E, rep. from * to end.
*14th row:* * 2B, 2M, 1B, 4E, 1B, 2M, rep. from * to last 8(0:4:8:0) sts., 2B, 2M, 1B, 3E(0:2B, 2M:2B, 2M, 1B, 3E:0).
*15th row:* 2E(0:1M, 1B, 2E:2E:0), * 1B, 2M, 1B, 2E, rep. from * to end.
*16th row:* 3E, 1B, * 2M, 2B, 2M, 1B, 4E, 1B, rep. from * to last 4(8:0:4:8) sts., 2M, 2B(2M, 2B, 2M, 1B, 1E:0:2M, 2B:2M, 2B, 2M, 1B, 1E).
*17th row:* as 11th.
*18th row:* G.
*19th row:* F.
*20th row:* * 3A, 1B, rep. from * to end.
*21st row:* * 1D, 1B, 1A, 1B, rep. from * to end.
*22nd row:* as 20th.
*23rd row:* M.
*24th row:* F.
*25th row:* B.
*26th row:* C.
*27th row:* B.
*28th row:* F.
*29th row:* G.
*30th row:* 1H, * 3J, 3H, rep. from * to last 1(5:3:1:5) sts., 1J(3J, 2H:3J:1J:3J, 2H).

*31st row:* 2J(0:1H, 3J:2J:0), * 3H, 3J, rep. from * to end.
*32nd row:* A.
*33rd row:* F.
*34th row:* * 7M, 3A, rep. from * to last 8(2:6:0:4) sts., 8(2:6:0:4:)M.
*35th row:* 9(3:7:1:5)M, * 3A, 7M, rep. from * to last 9 sts., 3A, 6M.
*36th row:* 2A, *1M, 9A, rep. from * to last 6(0:4:8:2) sts., 1M, 5A(0:1M, 3A:1M, 7A:2A).
*37th row:* 6(0:4:8:2)A, * 1M, 9A, rep. from * to last 2 sts., 1M, 1A.
*38th row:* 5M, * 3A, 7M, rep. from * to last 3(7:1:5:9) sts., 3A(3A, 4M:1A:3A, 2M:3A, 6M).
*39th row:* 1M(5M:2A, 7M:3M:7M), * 3A, 7M, rep. from * to last 7 sts., 3A, 4M.
*40th row:* H.
*41st row:* 1E, 2D(1D:3E, 2D:1E, 2D:1D), * 4E, 2D, rep. from * to last 5 sts., 4E, 1D.
*42nd row:* * 2D, 4E, rep. from * to last 2(0:4:2:0) sts., 2D(0:2D, 2E:2D:0).
*43rd row:* G.
*44th row:* F.

These 44 rows form patt.

Cont. in patt. until work measures same as back to underarm, ending with a p. row.

**Shape Armhole and Front**

Keeping patt. correct, cast off at beg. of next and alt. row 7 sts. once, and 4 sts. once.

Dec. 1 st. at armhole edge on next and foll. alt. row. 6(7:8:9:10) times, *at the same time*, when armhole measures 4 cm. (1½ in.) from beg., shape front by dec. 1st. at front edge on next and every foll. 3rd row until 28(30:32:34:36) sts. rem.

Cont. without shaping until armhole measures same as back to shoulder, ending at armhole edge.

**Shape Shoulder**

Cast off at beg. of next and every alt. row

7(8:8:9:9) sts. 3 times, and 7(6:8:7:9) sts. once.

## RIGHT FRONT

Work as given for left front, reversing patt. and all shapings.

## FRONT BORDER

Sew up shoulder and side seams.

Cast on 8 sts. with 2¼mm. needles and A. Work in k.1, p.1 rib, working 4 rows A, 4 rows F throughout.

Starting at centre of back, working towards right front, sew on border as worked. When bottom edge corner is reached, mitre as folls.:

* rib 6, turn, rib next row, rib 4, turn, rib next row, rib 2, turn, rib 4, turn, rib next row, rib 6, turn, rib next row *, rib all sts. Cont. around borders, marking position of 5 buttons on right front, and working buttonholes to correspond on left front as folls.:

*1st row:* work 3, cast off 3, work 1.
*2nd row:* work 2, cast on 3, work 3.

Work mitre shaping as from * to * above on lower left side corner.

When borders meet at centre back, cast off and sew border neatly tog.

## ARMBANDS

Cast on 8 sts. with 2¼mm. needles and A. Work in striped rib as for main border, to fit round armhole.

## MAKING UP

Press under a damp cloth with warm iron. Sew on arm borders, and sew border ends neatly together.

Neaten buttonhole edges.

Press seams.

Sew on buttons.

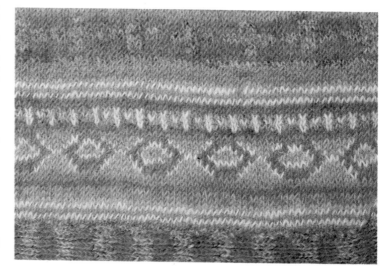

# Jacquard Rib Sleeveless Sweater

*1950*

*Fine, lightweight sleeveless sweater in simple, patterned rib, with round neck and ribbed hem, neck and armhole welts*

★★ Suitable for knitters with some previous experience

## MATERIALS

**Yarn**
Sunbeam 3 ply
8(8:9:9:10) × 25g. balls

**Needles**
1 pair 2mm.
1 pair 3mm.

## MEASUREMENTS

**Chest**
87(92:97:102:107) cm.
34(36:38:40:42) in.

**Length**
61(61:62:64:64) cm.
24(24:24¼:25:25) in.

## TENSION

36 sts. and 40 rows = 10 cm. (4 in.) square over patt. on 3mm. needles. If your tension square does not correspond to these measurements, adjust the needle size used.

## ABBREVIATIONS

k.=knit; p.=purl; st(s).=stitch(es); inc.= increase; dec.=decrease; beg.=begin(ning); rem. = remain(ing); rep. = repeat; alt. = alternate; tog. = together; sl. = slip stitch (transfer one stitch from left needle, knit-wise unless otherwise stated, to right hand needle.); cont. = continue; patt. = pattern; foll. = following; folls. = follows; mm. = millimetres; cm. = centimetres; in. = inch(es); st.st. = stocking stitch.

## BACK

Cast on 158(166:174:182:190) sts. with 2mm. needles.
*1st row:* * p.2, k.2, rep. from * to last 2 sts., p.2.
*2nd row:* * k.2, p.2, rep. from * to last 2 sts., k.2. Rep. 1st and 2nd rows for 9 cm. (3½ in.), ending with 2nd row.
Change to 3mm. needles and patt.
*1st row:* k.4(5:6:7:8), * p.2, k.1, p.4, k.4, p.4, k.1, p.2, k.4(5:6:7:8), rep. from * to end.

*2nd row:* p.4(5:6:7:8), * k.2, p.1, k.4, p.4, k.4, p.1, k.2, p.4(5:6:7:8), rep. from * to end.
*3rd row:* k.4(5:6:7:8), * p.2, k.1, p.3, k.6, p.3, k.1, p.2, k.4(5:6:7:8), rep. from * to end.
*4th row:* p.4(5:6:7:8), * k.2, p.1, k.3, p.6, k.3, p.1, k.2, p.4(5:6:7:8), rep. from * to end.
*5th row:* k.4(5:6:7:8), * p.3, k.1, p.2, k.6, p.2, k.1, p.3, k.4(5:6:7:8), rep. from * to end.

*6th row:* p.4(5:6:7:8), * k.3, p.1, k.2, p.6, k.2, p.1, k.3, p.4(5:6:7:8), rep. from * to end.
*7th row:* k.4(5:6:7:8), * p.3, k.1, p.1, k.8, p.1, k.1, p.3, k.4(5:6:7:8), rep. from * to end.
*8th row:* p.4(5:6:7:8), * k.3, p.1, k.1, p.8, k.1, p.1, k.3, p.4(5:6:7:8), rep. from * to end.
*9th row:* k.4(5:6:7:8), * p.2, k.1, p.1, k.10, p.1, k.1, p.2, k.4(5:6:7:8), rep. from * to end.
*10th row:* p.4(5:6:7:8), * k.2, p.1, k.1, p.10, k.1, p.1, k.2, p.4(5:6:7:8), rep. from * to end.
*11th row:* as 9th row.
*12th row:* as 10th row.
*13th row:* k.4(5:6:7:8), * p.1, k.1, p.1, k.4, p.4, k.4, p.1, k.1, p.1, k.4(5:6:7:8), rep. from * to end.
*14th row:* p.4(5:6:7:8), * k.1, p.1, k.1, p.4, k.4, p.4, k.1, p.1, k.1, p.4(5:6:7:8), rep. from * to end.
*15th, 17th and 19th rows:* as 13th row.
*16th, 18th and 20th rows:* as 14th row.
*21st and 23rd rows:* as 9th row.
*22nd and 24th rows:* as 10th row.
*25th row:* as 7th row.
*26th row:* as 8th row.
*27th row:* as 5th row.
*28th row:* as 6th row.
*29th row:* as 3rd row.
*30th row:* as 4th row.
*31st row:* as 1st row.
*32nd row:* as 2nd row.
These 32 rows form patt.
Work until back measures 40(40:40:41:41) cm. (15¾(15¾:15¾:16:16) in.) from beg., ending with a wrong side row.

**Shape Armholes**
Cast off 10(11:12:13:14) sts. at beg. of next 2 rows.
Now dec. 1 st. at each end of next row, and then every alt. row until 116(122:128:134:140) sts. rem.
Work until armholes measure 21(21:22:23:23) cm. (8¼(8¼:8½:9:9) in.) measured straight, ending with a wrong side row.

**Shape Shoulders and Neck Border**
Cast off 12(13:14:15:16) sts. at beg. of next 6 rows.
Change to 2mm. needles and cont. for neck border:

**Shape Shoulder**

Cast off 12(13:14:15:16) sts. at beg. of next row, and then the foll. alt. row.
Work 1 row.
Cast off 12(13:14:15:16) rem. sts.
Leave centre 20 sts. on a st. holder, rejoin yarn to neck edge of rem. sts. and patt. to end of row.
Work 1 row.
Cast off 3 sts. at beg. of next row, and then the 3 foll. alt. rows. Complete to match first side, working 1 row more, to end at armhole edge, before shaping shoulder.

**Neck Border**

With 2mm. needles and right side of work facing, k. up 42(42:42:44:44) sts. down left side of front neck edge, 20 sts. from st. holder, and 42(42:42:44:44) sts. up right side of neck.
*1st row:* k.1, p.2, * k.2, p.2, rep. from * to the last st., k.1.
*2nd row:* p.1, k.2, * p.2, k.2, rep. from * to the last st., p.1.
Rep. 1st and 2nd rows 5 times more.
Cast off in rib.

## MAKING UP AND ARMHOLE BORDERS

Press each piece lightly, following instructions on ball band.
Sew up shoulder and neck border seams.

**Armhole Borders**

With 2mm. needles and right side of work facing, k. up 176(176:184:192:196) sts. round armhole edge.
Work 12 rows in rib as for front neck border.
Cast off in rib.
Sew up side seams.
Press seams.

*1st row:* p.1, k.2, * p.2, k.2, rep. from * to last st., p.1.
*2nd row:* k.1, p.2, * k.2, p.2, rep. from * to last st., k.1.
Rep. 1st and 2nd rows 5 times more.
Cast off in rib.

## FRONT

Follow instructions for back until armhole shaping has been completed. Work until armholes measure 13(13:14:15:15) cm.

(5(5:5½:5¾:5¾) in.) measured on straight, ending with a wrong side row.

**Shape Neck**

*Next row:* patt. 48(51:54:57:60) sts., turn, leaving rem. sts. on spare needle.
Cont. on these sts.
Cast off 3 sts. at beg. of next row, and then the 3 foll. alt. rows.
Cont. on rem. 36(39:42:45:48) sts. until armhole measures same as back, ending at armhole edge.

# Diagonal Rib Slipover

*V-neck, sleeveless slipover in fine yarn, with shaped armholes and double-rib-pattern welts*

★★ Suitable for knitters with some previous experience

## MATERIALS

**Yarn**
Lister-Lee Motoravia 4 ply
4(4:5:5:6) × 50g. balls

**Needles**
1 pair 2¾mm.
1 pair 3¼mm.

## MEASUREMENTS

**Chest**
92(97:102:107:112) cm.
36(38:40:42:44) in.

**Length**
61(61:64:64:65) cm.
24(24:25:25:25½) in.

## TENSION

14 sts. and 18 rows = 5 cm. (2 in.) square over patt. on 3¼mm. needles. If your tension square does not correspond to these measurements, adjust the needle size used.

## ABBREVIATIONS

k.=knit; p.=purl; st(s).=stitch(es); inc.= increase; dec.=decrease; beg.=begin(ning); rem. = remain(ing); rep. = repeat; alt. = alternate; tog. = together; sl. = slip stitch (transfer one stitch from left needle, knitwise unless otherwise stated, to right hand needle.); cont. = continue; patt. = pattern; foll. = following; folls. = follows; mm. = millimetres; cm. = centimetres; in. = inch(es); st.st. = stocking stitch; sl.1K. = slip one stitch knitwise; sl.1P. = slip one stitch purlwise; y.fwd. = yarn forward; y.bk. = yarn back.

## BACK

** Cast on 128(136:144:152:160) sts. with 2¾mm. needles and work in rib as folls.:
*1st row* (right side): * k.2, p.2, rep. from * to end.
*2nd row:* as 1st row.
Rep. these two rows until work measures 10 cm. (4 in.). Change to 3¼mm. needles and work in patt. throughout as folls.:
*1st row:* k.1, * sl.1K., k.7, rep. from * to last 7 sts., sl.1K., k.6.
*2nd row:* p.6, * y.bk., sl.1P., y.fwd., p.7, rep. from * to last 2 sts., y.bk., sl.1P., y.fwd., p.1.
*3rd row:* k.2, * sl.1K., k.7, rep. from * to last 6 sts., sl.1K., k.5.
*4th row:* p.5, * y.bk., sl.1P., y.fwd., p.7, rep. from * to last 3 sts., y.bk., sl.1P., y.fwd., p.2.
*5th row:* k.3, * sl.1K., k.7, rep. from * to last 5 sts., sl.1K., k.4.
*6th row:* p.4, * y.bk., sl.1P., y.fwd., p.7, rep. from * to last 4 sts., y.bk., sl.1P., y.fwd., p.3.
*7th row:* k.4, * sl.1K., k.7, rep. from * to last 4 sts., sl.1K., k.3.

*8th row:* p.3, * y.bk., sl.1P., y.fwd., p.7, rep. from * to last 5 sts., y.bk., sl.1P., y.fwd., p.4.
*9th row:* k.5, * sl.1K., k.7, rep. from * to last 3 sts., sl.1K., k.2.
*10th row:* p.2., * y.bk., sl.1P., y.fwd., p.7, rep. from * to last 6 sts., y.bk., sl.1P., y.fwd., p.5.
*11th row:* k.6, * sl.1K., k.7, rep. from * to last 2 sts., sl.1K., k.1.
*12th row:* p.1,* y.bk., sl.1P., y.fwd., p.7, rep. from * to last 7 sts., y.bk., sl.1P., y.fwd., p.6.
*13th row:* * k.7., sl.1K., rep from * to end.
*14th row:* * y.bk., sl.1P., y.fwd., p.7, rep. from * to end.
*15th row:* * sl.1K., k.7, rep. from * to end.
*16th row:* * p.7., y.bk., sl.1P., y.fwd., rep. from * to end.

These 16 rows form the patt.

Cont. until back measures 33(33:36:36:36) cm. (13(13:14:14:14) in.) from beg., ending with a wrong side row.

### Shape Armholes

Cast off 10 sts. at beg. of next 2 rows, dec. 1 st. at both ends of next and every foll. alt. row 7(7:7:9:9) times.
[92(100:108:114:120) sts.] **
Work straight until back measures 60(60:62:62:63) cm. (23½(23½:24¼:24¼: 24¾) in.), ending with a wrong side row.

### Shape Shoulders

Cast off 6(7:8:9:10) sts. at beg. of next 4 rows.
Cast off 8(9:10:10:10) sts. at beg. of next 2 rows.
Put rem. 52(54:56:58:60) sts. onto a st. holder or a spare needle.

### FRONT

Work as for back from ** to **.
Work 4(4:4:0:0) rows straight.

### Shape Neck

Work 45(49:53:55:59) sts., turn, leaving rem. sts. on a spare needle.
Dec. 1 st. at neck edge on next and every foll. alt. row until 20(23:26:28:30) sts. rem.
Cont. straight until front measures same as back to shoulder shaping, ending with a wrong side row.

### Shape Shoulder

Cast off 6(7:8:9:10) sts. at beg. of next 2 alt. rows.
Cast off 8(9:10:10:10) sts. at beg. of next row.
Slip centre 2 sts. onto a safety pin for neckband, rejoin yarn to rem. sts. and work other half of front to match, reversing shapings.

### NECKBAND

Join right shoulder seam.
With 2¾mm. needles and right side facing, pick up and k. 62(62:62:62:66) sts. down left front, k. across 2 sts. left on pin, k. 64(62:64:66:68) sts. up right front and k. across 52(54:56:58:60) sts. at back.
[180(180:184:188:196) sts.]
*1st row:* (k.2, p.2) 28(28:29:30:31) times, k.2, p.2tog., p.2 (centre sts.), p.2 tog., * k.2, p.2, rep. from * 14(14:14:14:15) more times. Work 11 more rows in rib, dec. each side of centre 2 sts. on every row.
Cast off loosely in rib.

### ARMHOLE BAND

Sew up left shoulder seam.
With 2¾mm. needles, and right side facing, pick up and k.152(152:152:152:158) sts. around armhole and work in k.2., p.2 rib for 12 rows.
Cast off loosely in rib.

### MAKING UP

Press as advised on ball band.
Sew up neckband seam and side seams.

---

# Finely Patterned Polo-neck Sweater

## Long, loose sweater with generous raglan sleeves, ribbed welts and polo collar, in stocking stitch with patterned stripes

★★ Suitable for knitters with some previous experience

### MATERIALS

**Yarn**
Lister-Lee Motoravia 4 ply
11(12:12:13:14) × 50g. balls

**Needles**
1 pair of 2¼mm.
1 pair of 3mm.
1 set of double-pointed 2¼mm.
4 st. holders

### MEASUREMENTS

**Chest**
92(97:102:107:112) cm.
36(38:40:42:44) in.

**Length**
60(63:66:69:72) cm.
23¾(24¾:26:27:28¼) in.

**Sleeve Seam**
46 cm.
18 in.

### TENSION

30 sts. and 40 rows = 10 cm. (4 in.) square over patt. on 3mm. needles. If your tension square does not correspond to these measurements, adjust the needle size used.

### ABBREVIATIONS

k.=knit; p.=purl; st(s).=stitch(es); inc.= increas(ing); dec.=decreas(ing); beg.= begin(ning); rem.= remain(ing); rep. = repeat; alt. = alternate; tog. = together; sl. = slip (transfer one stitch from left needle, knitwise unless otherwise stated, to right hand needle.); cont. = continue; patt. = pattern; foll. = following; folls. = follows; mm. = millimetres; cm. = centimetres; in. = inches; st. st. = stocking st.: one row k., one row p.; g. st. = garter st.: every row k.; incs. = increases; decs. = decreases; p.s.s.o. = pass the sl. st. over.

### BACK

Cast on 160(168:176:184:192) sts. with 2¼mm. needles.
Work 8 cm. (3¼ in.) in k.1, p.1 rib.
Change to 3mm. needles and patt.

*1st row (right side)*: k.3, * k. into front and back of each of next 2 sts., k.6, rep. from * to last 5 sts., k. into front and back of each of next 2 sts., k.3.
*2nd row*: p.3, * p.2 tog. twice, p.6, rep. from * to last 7 sts., p.2 tog. twice, p.3.

These 2 rows form. patt.
NB When counting sts., disregard the extra sts. inc. in 1st patt. row.
Work in patt. until back measures 35(37:38:39:41) cm. (13¾(14½:15:15¼:16) in.), ending with a 2nd patt. row.

### Shape Raglans
Cast off 5 sts. at beg. of next 2 rows.
Dec. 1 st. at each end of next 5 rows.
Work 1 row.
* *9th row*: k.1, k. twice into each of next 2 sts., k.2 tog., work to last 5 sts., sl.1, k.1, p.s.s.o., k. twice into each of next 2 sts., k.1.
*10th row*: work to end, keeping patt. correct.
Rep. last 2 rows until 48(50:52:54:56) sts. rem.
Leave sts. on holder.

### FRONT
Work as for back until 78(80:82:84:86) sts. rem., ending with a p. row.

### Shape Neck
*1st row*: k.1, k. twice into each of next 2

sts., k.2 tog., work until there are 28 sts. on needle (not counting inc. sts.), turn. Finish this side first.
Work 1 row.
*3rd row*: k.1, k. twice into each of next 2 sts., k.2 tog., work to last 2 sts., k.2 tog.
Rep. last 2 rows until 6 sts. rem., ending with a p. row.
*Next row*: k.1, k. twice into each of next 2 sts., k.3 tog.
*Next row*: p.1, p.2 tog. twice, p.1.
*Next row*: k.1, k. twice into next st., k.2.
*Next row*: p.2 tog. twice, p.1.
*Next row*: k.1, k.2 tog.
Cast off.
Sl. centre 20(22:24:26:28) sts. onto holder.
Rejoin wool to rem. sts. and work to correspond with first side.

### SLEEVES
Cast on 80(80:88:88:96) sts. with 2¼mm. needles.
Work 8 cm. (3¼ in.) in k.1, p.1 rib.
Change to 3mm. needles and patt. as for back.
Work 4 rows.
Inc. 1 st. at each end of next and every 4th row until there are 132(138:144:150:156) sts., taking inc. sts. into patt.
Work straight until sleeve measures 46 cm. (18 in.), ending with a 2nd patt. row.

### Shape Raglan Top
Cast off 5 sts. at beg. of next 2 rows.
Dec. 1 st. at each end of next 7(2:9:4:3) rows.
Work 1(0:1:0:1) row, ending with 2nd patt. row.
Now work as for back from * until 18(22:16:20:22) sts. rem.
Leave sts. on holder.

### COLLAR
Sew up raglan seams.
With right side of work facing and double-pointed needles, k. up sts. round neck as folls.: (k.1, p.1) across 18(22:16: 20:22) sts. of left sleeve, k. up 30 sts. down side of neck, (k.1, p.1) across 20(22:24:26:28) sts. on holder at front, k. up 30 sts. up side of neck, (k.1, p.1) across 18(22:16:20:22) sts. of right sleeve and across 48(50:52:54:56) sts. of back neck. [164(176:168:180:188) sts.]
Work in rounds of k.1, p.1 rib for 15 cm. (5¾ in.).
Cast off loosely in rib.

### MAKING UP
Press lightly, avoiding rib.
Sew up side and sleeve seams.

# Twist-rib and Cable Sweater

*Round-neck, cable and twist-rib-pattern sweater with set-in sleeves, twist-rib welts and neckband*

★★ Suitable for knitters with some previous experience

## MATERIALS

**Yarn**
Hunter Shetland 2 ply
7(7:7:8) × 60g. hanks

**Needles**
1 pair 2¾mm.
1 pair 3¾mm.
1 cable needle
st. holder

## MEASUREMENTS

**Chest**
92(97:102:107) cm.
36(38:40:42) in.

**Length**
60(61:62:64) cm.
23½(24:24½:25) in.

**Sleeve Seam**
48(50:51:51) cm.
19(19½:20:20) in.

## TENSION

30 sts. and 36 rows = 10 cm. (4 in.) square over slightly stretched patt. on 3¾mm. needles. If your tension square does not correspond to these measurements, adjust the needle size used.

## ABBREVIATIONS

k. = knit; p. = purl; st(s). = stitch(es); inc. = increas(ing); dec. = decreas(ing); beg. = begin(ning); rem. = remain(ing); rep. = repeat; alt. = alternate; tog. = together; sl. = slip (transfer one stitch from left needle, knitwise unless otherwise stated, to right hand needle.); cont. = continue; patt. = pattern; foll. = following; folls. = follows; mm. = millimetres; cm. = centimetres; in. = inches; st. st. = stocking st.: one row k., one row p.; g. st. = garter st.: every row k.; incs. = increases; decs. = decreases; t.b.l. = through back of loop.

## FRONT

Cast on 144(150:158:164) sts. with 2¾mm. needles.
Work 26 rows in k.1 t.b.l., p.1, twist rib.
*Next row*: work in twist rib to last 2 sts., k.2 tog. [143(149:157:163) sts.]
*Next row*: beg. with a p. st., twist rib 15(11:15:11) sts., * inc. in next st., twist rib 13 sts. *, rep. from * to * to last 15(11:15:11) sts., inc. in next st., twist rib to end. [152(159:167:174) sts.]
Change to 3¾mm. needles.
Work in rib and cable patt. as folls.:
*1st row*: beg. with k.1 t.b.l., work 12(8:12:8) sts. in twist rib, * k.8, beg. with p.1, twist rib next 7 sts., * rep. from * to * to last 20(16:20:16) sts., k.8, beg. with p.1, twist rib to end.
*2nd row*: beg. with p.1, twist rib first 12(8:12:8) sts., * p.8, beg. with k.1 t.b.l., twist rib next 7 sts., * rep. from * to *, to last 20(16:20:16) sts., p.8, beg. with k.1 t.b.l., twist rib to end.

*3rd to 6th rows*: rep. 1st and 2nd rows twice more each.
*7th row*: beg. with k.1 t.b.l., work 12(8:12:8) sts. in twist rib, * sl. next 4 sts. onto cable needle and leave at front of work, k.4, k.4 from cable needle, beg. with p.1, twist rib next 7 sts., * rep. from * to * to last 5(1:5:1) sts., twist rib to end.
*8th row*: as 2nd.
These 8 rows form patt.
Rep. these 8 patt. rows 13(14:14:15) times more, then work rows 1 to 4 inclusive 1(0:1:0) times more.

**Shape Armholes**
Keeping patt. correct, cast off 6 sts. at beg. of next 2 rows.
Cast off 2 sts. at beg. of next 4 rows.
Now dec. 1 st. at beg. of every row until 118(127:131:142) sts. rem. **
Cont. straight in patt., working beg. and end 10(7:9:7) sts. of each row in twist rib until a total of 21½(22:22½:23) patts. have been worked.

**Shape Neck**
Work 52(56:58:63) sts., turn.
Work on these sts. first.
Cast off 4(5:5:6) sts. at beg. of next row.
Cast off 4(4:4:5) sts. at beg. of next 2 alt. rows.
Cast off 2 sts. at beg. of foll. 2 alt. rows, ending at armhole edge. [36(39:41:43) sts.]

**Shape Shoulder**
Cast off 12(13:13:14) sts. at beg. of next row and on the foll. alt. row.
Work 1 row, thus ending at armhole edge.
Cast off rem. 12(13:15:15) sts.
Sl. centre 14(15:15:16) sts. onto holder for neck.
Rejoin wool to rem. 52(56:58:63) sts., and work to match left side.

## BACK

Work as for front to **.
Cont. straight in patt. until 22½(23:23½: 24) patts. have been worked.
Work 2 more rows.

**Shape Shoulders**
Cast off 12(13:13:14) sts. at beg. of next 4 rows.
Cast off 12(13:15:15) sts. at beg. of next 2 rows.
Leave rem. 46(49:49:56) sts. on holder for back of neck.

## SLEEVES

Cast on 64(68:68:72) sts. with 2¾mm. needles.
Work 31 rows in twist rib.
*Next row*: working in twist rib, inc. 8 sts. evenly across row. [72(76:76:80) sts.]
Change to 3¾mm. needles and work in patt. as folls:
*1st row*: beg. with k.1 t.b.l., twist rib 2(4: 4:6) sts., k.8, * beg. p.1, twist rib 7, k.8, *, rep. from * to * to last 2(4:4:6) sts., beg. with p.1, twist rib to end.
This row sets patt.
With sts. as set, patt. 7 rows as for front.

Inc. 1 st. at each end of next and every foll. 6th row until there are 114(118:118: 122) sts.
N.B. Incorporate extra sts. into patt., after one extra cable appears at each side, work rem. inc. sts. in twist rib only.
Cont. straight in patt. until work measures 48(50:51:51) cm. 19(19½:20:20) in. or required length.

**Shape Top**
Cast off 6 sts. at beg. of next 2 rows.
Cast off 2 sts. at beg. of every row until 42(46:46:50) sts. rem.
Cast off.

## NECKBAND

Sew up left shoulder seam.
With 2¾mm. needles pick up and k.46 (49:49:56) sts. from back of neck, 32 sts. from shaped left front neck edge, 14(15: 15:16) sts. from centre front and 32 sts. from shaped right front neck edge. [124 (128:128:136) sts.]
Work 13 rows in twist rib.
Cast off in twist rib.

## MAKING UP

Sew up right shoulder seam, including neckband.
Sew up side and sleeve seams.
Set in sleeves.
Turn neckband in half onto wrong side and stitch.
Press lightly.

35

# Traditional, Shaped Waistcoat

*Firmly shadow-ribbed waistcoat with pockets and shaped hemline has mitred front border, sleeve and pocket borders in tubular rib*

★★ Suitable for knitters with some previous experience

## MATERIALS

**Yarn**
Patons Clansman 4 ply
7(7:8:9) × 50g. balls.

**Needles**
1 pair 3¼mm.

**Buttons**
5

## MEASUREMENTS

**Chest**
97(102:107:112) cm.
38(40:42:44) in.

**Length**
54(56:57:58) cm.
21¼(22:22¼:22¾) in.

## TENSION

30 sts. and 40 rows = 10 cm. (4 in.) square over patt. on 3¼mm. needles. If your tension square does not correspond to these measurements, adjust the needle size used.

## ABBREVIATIONS

k.=knit; p.=purl; st(s).=stitch(es); inc.= increase; dec.=decrease; beg.=begin(ning); rem. = remain(ing); rep. = repeat; alt. = alternate; tog. = together; sl. = slip stitch (transfer one stitch from left needle, knitwise unless otherwise stated, to right hand needle.); cont. = continue; patt. = pattern; foll. = following; folls. = follows; mm. = millimetres; cm. = centimetres; in. = inch(es); st.st. = stocking stitch; tw.2 = twist 2: k. into front of 2nd st., then front of first st. on left-hand needle, and sl. 2 sts. off needle tog.; y.fwd. = yarn forward; y.bk. = yarn back; sl.1P = sl. 1 st. purlwise.
N.B. The stitch used for the main part has a tendency to pull sideways and must be pressed straight when the garment is finished.

## BACK

Cast on 121(127:133:139) sts. and work in patt. as folls.:
*1st row:* k.1, * (tw.2) twice, p.1, k.1, rep. from * to end.

*2nd row:* p.
These 2 rows form patt.
Work straight in patt. for 8 rows.

**Shape Sides**
Inc. 1 st. at each end of next and every foll. 4th row until there are 145(153:161:169) sts., taking inc. sts. into patt.
Work straight in patt. until back measures 30 cm. (11¾ in.), ending with right side facing.

**Shape Armholes**
Cast off 6(7:8:9) sts. at beg. of next 2 rows.
Dec. 1 st. at each end of next and every foll. alt. row until 115(121:123:129) sts. rem.
Work straight until armhole measures 24(26:27:28) cm. (9½(10¼:10½:11) in.), ending with right side facing.

**Shape Shoulders**
Cast off 6 sts. at beg. of next 10(6:4:2) rows, then 7 sts. at beg. of foll. 0(4:6:8) rows.
Cast off rem. 55(57:57:61) sts.

## POCKET LININGS (2)

Cast on 45 sts. and work in st.st. for 9 cm. (3½ in.), ending with a k. row.
Leave sts. on a spare needle.

## RIGHT FRONT

Cast on 7 sts. and work 2 rows in patt. as for back.
*3rd row:* k. twice into first st., work to last st., k. twice into last st.
*4th row:* p. twice into first st., work to end.

Rep. last 2 rows until there are 40 sts., taking inc. sts. into patt.
*Next row:* k. twice into first st., work to end.
*Next row:* cast on 6 sts., p. to end.
Rep. last 2 rows 3 times more. [68 sts.]
*Next row:* work to end.
*Next row:* cast on 5(11:17:23) sts., p. to end. [73(79:85:91) sts.]
Place marker at end of last row.
Work straight in patt. until front measures 9 cm. (3½ in.) from marker, ending with a wrong side row.

**Place Pocket Lining**
*Next row:* patt. 14(17:20:23), cast off next 45 sts., patt. to end.
*Next row:* work to cast off sts., in place of these p. across sts. of pocket lining, p. to end.
Work straight in patt. until side front from marker upwards, matches back to armhole, ending with a right side row.

**Shape Armhole and Front Slope**
*Next row:* cast off 6(7:8:9), work to end.
Dec. 1 st. at each end of next and every foll. alt. row until 47(52:53:58) sts. rem.
Work 1 row.
Cont. dec. 1 st. at front slope on every alt. row until 46(49:50:49) sts. rem.
Work 1 row.
Dec. 1 st. at front slope on next and every foll. 4th row until 30(32:33:34) sts. rem.
Work straight until armhole matches back to shoulder, ending with a right side row.

**Shape Shoulder**
Cast off 6 sts. at beg. of next and foll. 3(2:1:0) alt. rows. Work 1 row.
Cast off 7 sts. at beg. of foll. 0(1:2:3) alt. rows. Work 1 row.
Cast off rem. 6(7:7:7) sts.

## LEFT FRONT

Work as for right front, reversing shapings.

## MAKING UP AND BORDERS

Block and press, following instructions on ball band.
Sew up shoulder seams.
Sew up side seams.

**Front Border**
Cast on 16 sts. and work as folls.:
*1st row:* * k.1, y.fwd., sl.1P, y.bk., rep. from * to end.
Rep. this row throughout.

Work straight until border, starting at right side seam, fits along right front edge from side to point.

**Work mitre**

*1st row:* work to last 2 sts., turn.
*2nd and every alt. row:* work to end.
*3rd row:* work to last 4 sts., turn.
*5th row:* work to last 6 sts., turn.
Cont. in this way, working 2 sts. less on every alt. row until 2 sts. rem.
Now work 2 sts. more on every alt. row until all sts. are worked.
Work straight until strip fits up to marker.

**Work half mitre**

*1st row:* work to last 6 sts., turn.
*2nd row:* work to end.
*3rd row:* work to last 12 sts., turn.
*4th row:* work to end.
*5th row:* work to last 6 sts., turn.
*6th row:* work to end.
Work straight until strip fits up front to start of front slope shaping.
Work half mitre again.
Work straight until strip fits around to centre back of neck.
Cast off.
Work 2nd front border to match, beg. at right side seam and working across lower edge of back, before working around front. Mark the positions of 5 buttons between half mitres on right front, with lowest button 3 cm. (1¼ in.) above lower half mitre, and work buttonholes as folls.:
*1st row:* work 6, cast off 4 sts., work to end.
*Next row:* patt. to cast off sts., cast on 4, patt. to end.
Complete to match first border.

**Armhole Border**

Cast on 14 sts. and work in patt. as for front border until border fits around armhole when very slightly stretched. Cast off.

**Pocket Edge and Finishing**

Cast on 16 sts. and work in patt. as given for front border until strip fits along pocket cast off sts. when slightly stretched. Cast off.
Stitch sides of pocket edges neatly to right side of work, and pocket linings to wrong side.
Sew armhole borders around armholes.
Sew front borders to waistcoat, allowing them to overlap main work slightly to give a neat finish.
Sew on buttons.

# Sleeveless Pullover in Brick Stitch 1942

*Hip-length, sleeveless pullover with V-neck in brick stitch with garter stitch neck border and bias, garter stitch sleeve borders*

★★ Suitable for knitters with some previous experience

## MATERIALS

Sirdar Country Style 4 ply
4(4:5:5) × 50g. balls

**Needles**
1 pair 2¾mm.
1 pair 3¼mm.

## MEASUREMENTS

**Chest**
97(102:107:112) cm.
38(40:42:44) in.

**Length**
59(61:63:65) cm.
23¼(24:24¾:25½) in.

## TENSION

28sts. and 36 rows = 10 cm. (4 in.) square over patt. with 3¼mm. needles. If your tension square does not correspond to these measurements, adjust the needle size used.

## ABBREVIATIONS

k. = knit; p. = purl; st(s). = stitch(es); inc. = increas(ing); dec. = decreas(ing); beg. = begin(ning); rem. = remain(ing); rep. = repeat; alt. = alternate; tog. = together; sl. = slip (transfer one stitch from left needle, knitwise unless otherwise stated, to right hand needle.); cont. = continue; patt. = pattern; foll. = following; folls. = follows; mm. = millimetres; cm. = centimetres; in. = inches; st. st. = stocking st.: one row k., one row p.; g. st. = garter st.: every row k.; incs. = increases; decs. = decreases; m.1 = make 1 st.: pick up horizontal loop lying before next st. and k. into back of it.

## BACK

*** Cast on 128(131:134:137) sts. with 2¾mm. needles and work in rib as folls.:
*1st row (right side):* * k.2, p.1, rep. from * to last 2 sts., k.2.
*2nd row:* p.2, * k.1, p.2, rep. from * to end.
Rep. these 2 rows until rib measures 8 cm. (3¼ in.) from cast-on edge, ending

with a 2nd row.
*Next row:* rib 4(8:2:10), m.1, (rib 6(5:5:4), m.1) 20(23:26:29) times, rib to end. [149(155:161:167) sts.]
Change to 3¼mm. needles.
K. 1 row.
Cont. in patt.:
*1st row (right side):* * p.5, k.1, rep. from * to last 5 sts., p.5.
*2nd row:* k.5, * p.1, k.5, rep. from * to end.
*3rd and 5th rows:* as 1st.
*4th and 6th rows:* as 2nd.
*7th row:* p.2, * k.1, p.5, rep. from * to last 3 sts., k.1, p.2.
*8th row:* k.2, p.1, * k.5, p.1, rep. from * to last 2 sts., k.2.
*9th and 11th rows:* as 7th.
*10th and 12th rows:* as 8th.
These 12 rows form patt.
Cont. straight in patt. until back measures 38(39:40:41) cm. (15(15¼:15¾: 16) in.) from cast-on edge, ending with a wrong side row. ***

**Shape Armholes**
Cast off 8(10:11:12) sts. at beg. of next 2 rows.
Dec. 1 st. at each end of next and every foll. alt. row until 117(121:125:129) sts. rem.
Cont. on rem. sts. in patt. until armholes measure 21(22:23:24) cm. (8¼(8½:9:9½) in.) from beg. of armhole shaping, ending with a wrong side row.

**Shape Shoulders**
Cast off 18(19:20:21) sts. at beg. of next 2 rows.
Cast off 18(18:17:17) sts. at beg. of foll. 2 rows.
Cast off rem. 45(47:51:53) sts.

## FRONT

Work as for back from *** to ***

**Shape Armholes**
Cast off 8(10:11:12) sts. at beg. of next 2 rows.
Dec. 1 st. at each end of next row and foll. 2 alt. rows, then work 1 row. [127(129: 133:137) sts.]

**Shape Neck**
*Next row:* patt. 2 tog., patt. 61(62:64:66) sts., turn, leave rem. sts. on a spare needle.

Dec. 1 st. at neck edge on next and every foll. 3rd row 22(23:25:26) times in all, AT THE SAME TIME cont. to shape armhole until 8(7:7:7) decs. in all have been worked. [36(37:37:38) sts.]
Work straight on rem. sts. until the same number of rows have been worked as for back to shoulder shaping, ending at armhole edge.

### Shape Shoulder
Cast off 18(19:20:21) sts. at beg. of next row.
Work 1 row.
Cast off rem. sts.
Return to sts. on spare needle, cast off centre st., rejoin yarn and complete right half of neck line as left half, reversing all shapings.

## NECKBAND
Sew up shoulder seams.
Cast on 1 st. with 2¾mm. needles.
*1st row (right side):* k.1.
*2nd row:* k. into front and back of st.
*3rd row:* k.2.
*4th row:* inc. 1 st., k.1.
Cont. in g. st., inc. 1 st. at same edge on every alt. row until there are 12 sts.
Work straight on all sts. in g. st. until band fits left side of neck to centre back neck, with point to centre front, and band slightly stretched.
Count number of rows worked on all sts., and work that number of rows again.
Dec. 1 st. at shaped edge on every alt. row until 1 st. rem.
Fasten off.

## ARMHOLE BANDS
Cast on 12 sts. with 2¾mm. needles and k. 1 row.
Work as folls.:
*1st row:* inc. 1 st., k.9, k.2 tog.
*2nd row:* k.2 tog., k. to last st., m.1, k.1.
Rep. these 2 rows until bias band fits armhole when slightly stretched.
Cast off.
Make another band in the same way.

## MAKING UP
Using a flat seam, neatly sew on armhole bands.
Sew up side and armhole band seams.
Sew on neckband with a flat seam.
Do not press.

---

# Cable and Rib Sweater

*1953*

## Chunky sports sweater with set-in sleeves, knitted in alternating bands of cable stitch and ribbing

★★ Suitable for knitters with some previous experience

## MATERIALS
### Yarn
Jaeger Luxury Spun DK
11(11:12:12:13) × 50g. balls.

### Needles
1 pair 3mm.
1 pair 3¾mm.
1 cable needle

## MEASUREMENTS
### Chest
92(97:102:107:112) cm.
36(38:40:42:44) in.

### Length
65(66:67:68:69) cm.
25½(26:26¼:26¾:27¼) in.

### Sleeve Seam
48(48:49:49:50) cm.
18¾(18¾:19¼:19¼:19½) in.

## TENSION
29 sts. and 27 rows = 10 cm. (4 in.) square over patt. on 3¾mm. needles, slightly flattened as in wear. If your tension square does not correspond to these measurements, adjust the needle size used.

## ABBREVIATIONS
k.=knit; p.=purl; st(s).=stitch(es); inc.=

increase; dec.=decrease; beg.=begin(ning); rem.=remain(ing); rep.=repeat; alt.=alternate; tog.=together; sl.=slip stitch (transfer one stitch from left needle, knitwise unless otherwise stated, to right hand needle.); cont.=continue; patt.=pattern; foll.=following; folls.=follows; mm.=millimetres; cm.=centimetres; in.=inch(es); st.st.=stocking stitch; p.f.b.=p. into front and back of ext st.; C10B=cable 10 back: sl. next 5 sts. onto cable needle, leave at back, k.5, then k.5 from cable needle.

## BACK
Cast on 117(127:135:145:153) sts. with 3mm. needles and work in single rib beg. and ending right side rows with p.1 and wrong side rows with k.1.
Cont. until work measures 8 cm. (3¼ in.) from beg., ending with a right side row.
*Inc. row:* (k.1, p.1) 8(9:11:12:11) times, k.1, * p.f.b. 5 times, (k.1, p.1) 10(11:11:12:14) times, k.1, rep. from * to last 22(24:28:30:28) sts., p.f.b. 5 times, (k.1, p.1) 8(9:11:12:11) times, k.1. [137(147:155:165:173) sts.]
Change to 3¾mm. needles and patt.
*1st row:* rib 17(19:23:25:23), thus ending p.1, * k.10, rib 21(23:23:25:29), rep. from * to last 27(29:33:35:33) sts., k.10, rib 17(19:23:24:23).
*2nd row:* rib 17(19:23:25:23), * p.10, rib 21(23:23:25:29), rep. from * to last 27(29:33:35:33) sts., p.10, rib 17(19:23:25:23).
Rep. these 2 rows twice more.
*7th row:* rib 17(19:23:25:23), * C10B, rib 21(23:23:25:29), rep. from * to last 27(29:33:

35:33) sts., C10B, rib 17(19:23:25:23).
*8th row:* as 2nd.
*9th row to 12th row:* rep. 1st to 2nd rows twice more.
These 12 rows form one patt.
Cont. in patt. until work measures 43(44:44:45:45) cm. (16¾(17¼:17¼:17¾:17¾) in.) from beg., ending with a wrong side row.

**Shape Armholes**
Cast off 4 sts. at beg. of next 2 rows.
Cast off 2 sts. at beg. of next 6(6:8:10:12) rows.
Cast off 1 st. at beg. of next 8(12:12:12:12) rows.
Cont. on rem. 109(115:119:125:129) sts. until armholes measure 22(22:23:23:24) cm. (8½(8½:9:9:9½) in.) measured on the straight, ending with a wrong side row.

**Shape Shoulders**
Cast off 8(8:8:9:9) sts. at beg. of next 6 rows, then cast off 7(9:11:10:12) sts. at beg. of next 2 rows.
Cast off rem. 47(49:49:51:51) sts.

## FRONT

Work as for back until you have worked 22 rows fewer that on back to start of shoulder, ending with a wrong side row.

**Shape Neck and Shoulders**
*Next row:* patt. 47(49:51:53:55) sts. and leave these sts. of left front on a spare needle, cast off next 15(17:17:19:19) sts., patt. to end.
Cont. on 47(49:51:53:55) sts. now rem. on needle for right front and work 1 row straight.
** Cast off 4 sts. at beg. of next row, 2 sts. at same edge on next 3 alt. rows and 1 st. on next 6 alt. rows.
Work 2 rows on rem. 31(33:35:37:39) sts., thus ending at armhole edge.
Cast off 8(8:8:9:9) sts. at beg. of next row and next 2 alt. rows.
Work 1 row, then cast off rem. 7(9:11:10:12) sts.
Rejoin yarn to neck edge of left front sts. Complete as for right front from * to end, reversing shapings.

## SLEEVES

Cast on 57(59:63:65:65) sts. with 3mm. needles and work in rib as on back welt for 8 cm. (3¼ in.), ending with a right side row.
*Inc. row:* rib 13(13:15:15:13), * p.f.b. 5 times, rib 21(23:23:25:29), p.f.b. 5 times, rib 13(13:15:15:13). [67(69:73:75:75) sts.]
Change to 3¾mm. needles and patt.
*1st row:* rib 13(13:15:15:13), k.10, rib 21(23:23:25:29), k.10, rib 13(13:15:15:13).
Cont. in patt. as now set, working cables over the 2 groups of 10 sts., but at same time work 4 more rows straight, then inc. 1 st. at both ends of next row, then every foll. 6th row 5(7:5:7:2) times, then inc. at both ends of every foll. 4th row 16(13:16:13:21) times keeping all extra sts. in rib.
Cont. on these 111(111:117:117:123) sts. until work measures 48(48:49:49:50) cm. (18¾(18¾:19¼:19¼:19½) in.) from beg.

**Shape Top**
Cast off 4 sts. at beg. of next 2 rows, 2 sts. at beg. of next 6(6:8:10:12) rows, 1 st. at beg. of next 8(12:12:12:14) rows, 2 sts. at beg. of next 8(6:6:4:6) rows, 4 sts. at beg. of next 8(8:6:6:4) rows and 5 sts. at beg. of next 2(2:4:4:6) rows.
Cast off rem. 25 sts.

## NECKBAND

Sew up right shoulder seam matching patt. With right side of work facing you and 3mm. needles, pick up and k.71(73:73:75:75) sts. round front neck edge and 42(44:44:46:46) sts. across back neck.
Work in rib as on welt for 9 rows.
Cast off loosely ribwise.

## MAKING UP

Sew up left shoulder seam and ends of neckband.
Sew in sleeves, then sew up side and sleeve seams.

---

# Mock Cable Sweater

1958

***Guernsey wool, V-neck sweater in a mock cable pattern, with set-in sleeves and single-ribbed welts***

★★ Suitable for knitters with some previous experience

## MATERIALS

**Yarn**
Poppleton Guernsey 5 ply
6(7:7:8:8) × 100g. balls

**Needles**
1 pair 2¾mm.
1 pair 3¼mm.
1 set of 4 double-pointed 2¾mm.

## MEASUREMENTS

**Chest**
92(97:102:107:112) cm.
36(38:40:42:44) in.

**Length**
64(65:67:68:69) cm.
25(25½:26¼:26¾:27) in.

**Sleeve Seam**
46(47:48:48:49) cm.
18(18½:18¾:18¾:19¼) in.

## TENSION

30 sts. and 35 rows = 10 cm. (4 in.) square over patt. on 3¼mm. needles. If your tension square does not correspond to these measurements, adjust the needle size used.

## ABBREVIATIONS

k.=knit; p.=purl; st(s).=stitch(es); inc.=increase; dec.=decrease; beg.=begin(ning); rem. = remain(ing); rep. = repeat; alt. = alternate; tog. = together; sl. = slip stitch (transfer one stitch from left needle, knitwise unless otherwise stated, to right hand needle.); cont. = continue; patt. = pattern; foll. = following; folls. = follows; mm. = millimetres; cm. = centimetres; in. = inch(es); st.st. = stocking stitch; p.s.s.o. = pass slipped stitch over.

## BACK

** Cast on 131(137:143:149:155) sts. with 2¾mm. needles.
*1st row:* k.2, * p.1, k.1, rep. from * to last st., k.1.
*2nd row:* * k.1, p.1, rep. from * to last st., k.1.
Rep. 1st and 2nd rows for 10 cm. (4 in.), ending with 2nd row.
*Next row:* k.10(8:8:10:5), * k. twice into next st., k.10(9:8:7:7), rep. from * to last 11(9:9:11:6) sts., k. twice into next st., k. to end. [142(150:158:166:174) sts.]
Change to 3¼mm. needles and patt.
*1st row* (wrong side): * k.2, p.2, rep. from * to last 2 sts., k.2.
*2nd row:* * p.2, k.2, rep. from * to last 2 sts., p.2.

*3rd row:* as 1st row.

*4th row:* * p.2, take the needle in front of first st. on left hand needle and k. the 2nd st., keeping needle at front, now k. the first st., sl. both sts. off the needle tog., rep. from * to last 2 sts., p.2.

These 4 rows form patt.

Work until back measures 42(42:43:44:46) cm. (16½(16½:16¾:17¼:18) in.) from beg., ending with a wrong side row. **

### Shape Armholes

Cast off 5(6:7:8:9) sts. at beg. of next 2 rows.

Now dec. 1 st. at each end of next 3 rows, and then the 5(6:7:7:7) following alt. rows. [116(120:124:130:136) sts.]

Work until armholes measure 22(23:23: 24:24) cm. (8½(9:9:9½:9½) in.) measured straight, ending with a wrong side row.

### Shape Shoulders

Cast off at beg. of next and foll. rows, 8 sts. 8 times, and 5(6:7:8:9) sts. twice.

Slip rem. 42(44:46:50:54) sts. onto a st. holder.

### FRONT

Follow instructions for back from ** to **.

### Shape Armholes and Neck

*Next row:* cast off 5(6:7:8:9) sts., patt. 66(69:72:75:78) sts. including st. on needle, turn, leaving rem. sts. on spare needle.

Cont. on these sts.

*Next row:* k.2 tog., work to end.

Cont. to dec. for neck on every 3rd row, and at the same time dec. 1 st. at armhole edge on the next 3 rows, and then the 5(6: 7:7:7) foll. alt. rows.

Now keeping armhole edge straight, cont. to dec. for neck on every 3rd row until 37(38:39:40:41) sts. rem.

Work until armhole measures same as back, ending at armhole edge.

### Shape Shoulder

Cast off at beg. of next and foll. alt. rows, 8 sts. 4 times.

Work 1 row.

Cast off 5(6:7:8:9) rem. sts.

Rejoin yarn to rem. sts. at neck edge, patt. to end.

*Next row:* cast off 5(6:7:8:9) sts., patt. to last 2 sts., k.2 tog. Complete to match first side, working 1 row more to end at armhole edge before shaping shoulder.

### SLEEVES

Cast on 63(63:67:67:71) sts. with 2¾mm. needles and work 8 cm. (3 in.) in rib as for back.

*Next row:* k.1(3:3:5) * k. twice into next st., k.5, rep. from * to last 2(2:4:4:6) sts., k. twice into next st., k.1(3:3:5). [74(74:78: 78:82) sts.]

Change to 3¼mm. needles and patt.

Work 4 rows.

Inc. 1 st. at each end of next row, and then every 6th(6th:6th:5th:5th) row until there are 106(112:118:124:130) sts.

Work until sleeve measures 46(47:48: 48:49) cm. (18(18½:18¾:18¾:19¼) in.) from beg., ending with a wrong side row.

### Shape Top

Cast off 5(6:7:8:9) sts. at beg. of next 2 rows.

Now dec. 1 st. at each end of every row until 86(86:90:90:94) sts. rem., and then every alt. row until 58 sts. rem.

Cast off at beg. of next and foll. rows, 2 sts. twice, 3 sts. twice, 4 sts. twice, and 5 sts. 4 times.

Cast off rem. 20 sts.

### MAKING UP AND NECK BORDER

Press each piece lightly, foll. instructions on ball band.

Sew up shoulder seams.

### Neck Border

With right side of work facing, and double-pointed needles, k. up sts. round neck as folls.:

1st needle – 42(44:46:50:54) sts. from holder at back, 2nd needle – 70(74:78: 82:86) sts. down left side of neck to centre front, 3rd needle – 69(73:77:81:85) sts. up right side of neck. [181(187:201:213:225) sts.]

*1st round:* 1st needle – (k.1, p.1) to end; 2nd needle – (k.1, p.1) to last 2 sts., sl.1, k.1, p.s.s.o.; 3rd needle – k.2 tog., (p.1, k.1) to last st., p.1.

*2nd round:* 1st needle – (k.1, p.1) to end; 2nd needle – (k.1, p.1) to last st., k.1; 3rd needle – k.1, (p.1, k.1) to last st., p.1.

*3rd round:* 1st needle – (k.1, p.1) to end; 2nd needle – (k.1, p.1) to last 3 sts., k.1, sl.1, k.1, p.s.s.o.; 3rd needle – k.2 tog., (k.1, p.1) to end.

*4th round:* 1st needle – (k.1, p.1) to end; 2nd needle – (k.1, p.1) to end; 3rd needle – (p.1, k.1) to last st., p.1.

Rep. last 4 rounds twice more.

Cast off firmly in rib.

Sew up side and sleeve seams.

Sew sleeves into armholes.

Press seams.

---

# Three-coloured Striped Socks

*Simple socks in stocking stitch stripes with ribbed welts and adjustable length*

★★ Suitable for knitters with some previous experience

### MATERIALS

**Yarn**

Rowan 3 ply Botany
4 × 25g. hanks Main Col. A
1 × 25g. hank Col. B
1 × 25g. hank Col. C

**Needles**

1 pair 2¾mm.
1 set of 4 double-pointed 2¾mm.
3 st. holders

### MEASUREMENTS

**Foot Length (adjustable)**
from 24 cm.
9½ in.

**Length from Top to Base of Heel**
28 cm. approx.
11 in. approx.

### TENSION

36 sts. and 44 rows = 10 cm. (4 in.) square over st. st. on 2¾mm. needles. If your tension square does not correspond to

these measurements, adjust the needle size used.

### ABBREVIATIONS

k.=knit; p.=purl; st(s).=stitch(es); inc.= increas(ing); dec.=decreas(ing); beg.= begin(ning); rem. = remain(ing); rep. = repeat; alt. = alternate; tog. = together; sl. = slip (transfer one stitch from left needle, knitwise unless otherwise stated, to right hand needle.); cont. = continue; patt. = pattern; foll. = following; folls. =

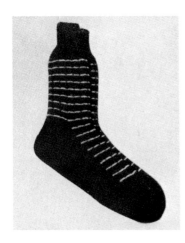

follows; mm. = millimetres; cm. = centimetres; in. = inches; st. st. = stocking st.: one row k., one row p.; g. st. = garter st.: every row k.; incs. = increases; decs. = decreases; p.s.s.o. = pass the sl. st. over; sl.1p. = sl. 1 purlwise.

Cast on 64 sts. with 2¾mm. needles and A.
Work in k.2, p.2 rib for 8 cm. (3¼ in.)
*Inc. row*: k.3, * k. twice into next st., k.6, rep. from * to last 5 sts., k. twice into next st., k.4. [73 sts.]
Work in patt. as folls., carrying yarns not in use loosely up sides of work.
*1st row (wrong side)*: p.
*2nd row*: * p.1, k.5, rep. from * to last st., p.1.
*3rd row*: * k.1, p.5, rep. from * to last st., k.1.
Rep. last 2 rows twice more.
*8th row*: with B, as 2nd.
*9th row*: with C, p.
*10th row*: with A, k.
*11th row*: with A, as 3rd.
*12th row*: with A, as 2nd.
Rep. last 2 rows twice more.
*17th row*: with B, as 3rd.
*18th row*: with C, k.
These 18 rows form patt.
Work until sock measures approx. 23 cm. (9 in.) from beg., ending with a 10th row.
Break off all 3 colours.

### Divide for Heel
*Next row (wrong side)*: sl. first 18 sts. onto a holder for heel, join in A and k.1, * p.5, k.1, rep. from * 5 times more.
Sl. rem. 18 sts. onto 2nd holder for heel.

### Instep
Cont. working in patt. on rem. 37 instep sts. for 18 cm. (7 in.), ending on wrong side with A.
Break yarn and sl. sts. onto a holder.

### Shape Heel
With wrong side facing, sl. 36 heel sts. onto one needle.
Join in A.
*1st row*: sl.1p., p. to end.
*2nd row*: keeping yarn at back, sl.1p., k.1, rep. from * to end.
Rep. last 2 rows 17 times more.

### Turn Heel
*1st row*: sl.1, p.20, p.2 tog., p.1, turn.
*2nd row*: sl.1, k.7, sl.1, k.1, p.s.s.o., k.1, turn.
*3rd row*: sl.1, p.8, p.2 tog., p.1, turn.
*4th row*: sl.1, k.9, sl.1, k.1, p.s.s.o., k.1, turn.
*5th row*: sl.1, p.10, p.2 tog., p.1, turn.
Cont. to dec. in this way, working 1 more st. before the dec. on each row until 22 sts. rem.
Pick up 18 sts. down each side of heel and arrange these sts. and heel sts. onto 1 needle.
*1st row*: k.1, sl.1, k.1, p.s.s.o., k. to last 3 sts., k.2 tog., k.1.
*2nd row*: p.
Rep. last 2 rows until 36 sts. rem.
Cont. in st. st. until sole measures same as instep ending with a p. row.
With set of 4 double-pointed needles divide sole sts. onto 2 needles.

With 3rd needle, k. across instep sts., dec. 1 st. in centre of row. [72 sts.]
Work in the round until foot measures 19 cm. (7½ in.) or 5 cm. (2 in.) less than desired length.

### Shape Toe
*Next round*: 1st needle – k.1, sl.1, k.1, p.s.s.o., k. to end, 2nd needle – k. to last 3 sts., k.2 tog., k.1, 3rd needle – k.1, sl.1, k.1, p.s.s.o., k. to last 3 sts., k.2 tog., k.1.
K. 1 round.
Rep. last 2 rounds until 20 sts. rem.
Sl. sts. from first needle onto second needle.
Cast off sts. from two needles tog.: hold 2 needles parallel and cast off 1 st. from each needle alternately to end.

### MAKING UP

Sew up back and foot seams.

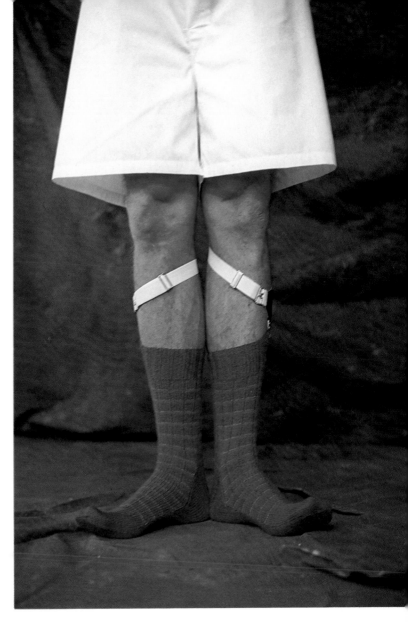

# V-neck, Sleeveless Cabled Pullover 1957

*Long slipover with front and back cable panels, V-neck and ribbed welts*

★★ Suitable for knitters with some previous experience

## MATERIALS

**Yarn**
Wendy Pampas
4(5:5:5) × 50g. balls

**Needles**
1 pair 3mm.
1 pair 3¾mm.
cable needle

## MEASUREMENTS

**Chest**
92(97:102:107) cm.
36(38:40:42) in.

**Length**
63(65:67:68) cm.
24¾(25½:26¼:26¾) in.

## TENSION

24 sts. and 32 rows = 10 cm. (4 in.) square over st. st. on 3¾mm. needles. If your tension square does not correspond to these measurements, adjust the needle size used.

## ABBREVIATIONS

k. = knit; p. = purl; st(s). = stitch(es); inc. = increas(ing); dec. = decreas(ing); beg. = begin(ning); rem. = remain(ing); rep. = repeat; alt. = alternate; tog. = together; sl. = slip (transfer one stitch from left needle, knitwise unless otherwise stated, to right hand needle.); cont. = continue; patt. = pattern; foll. = following; folls. = follows; mm. = millimetres; cm. = centimetres; in. = inches; st. st. = stocking st.: one row k., one row p.; g. st. = garter st.: every row k.; incs. = increases; decs. = decreases; C8F = cable 8 front: sl. the next 4 sts. onto cable needle and hold at front of work, k. 4 sts., k. sts. from cable needle; t.b.l. = through back of loops; m.1 = make 1 st.: pick up horizontal loop lying before next st. and k. into the front of it.

## BACK

Cast on 118(124:130:136) sts. with 3mm. needles.
Work 8 cm. (3¼ in.) in k.1, p.1 rib, ending with a right side row.
*Inc. row (wrong side):* rib 23(25:27:29), m.1, rib 2, m.1, rib 5, m.1, rib 2, m.1, rib 5, m.1, rib 2, m.1, rib 40(42:44:46), m.1, rib 2, m.1, rib 5, m.1, rib 2, m.1, rib 5, m.1, rib 2, m.1, rib 23(25:27:29) sts. [130(136: 142:148) sts.]
Change to 3¾mm. needles.
Work in reverse st. st. with cable panels as folls.:

*1st row (right side):* p.21(23:25:27), k.8, p.1, k.8, p.1, k.8, p.36(38:40:42), k.8, p.1, k.8, p.1, k.8, p.21(23:25:27).
*2nd row:* k.21(23:25:27), p.8, k.1, p.8, k.1, p.8, k.36(38:40:42), p.8, k.1, p.8, k.1, p.8, k.21(23:25:27).
*3rd row:* p.21(23:25:27), C8F, p.1, k.8, p.1, C8F, p.36(38:40:42), C8F, p.1, k.8, p.1, C8F, p.21(23:25:27).
*4th row:* as 2nd.
*5th and 6th rows:* as 1st and 2nd.
*7th row:* p.21(23:25:27), C8F, p.1, C8F, p.1, C8F, p.36(38:40:42), C8F, p.1, C8F, p.1, C8F, p.21(23:25:27).
*8th row:* as 2nd.
These 8 rows form patt.
Cont. straight in patt. until work measures 36(38:39:40) cm. (14(15:15¼: 15¾) in.), ending with a wrong side row.

**Shape Armholes**
Cast off 7(8:10:11) sts. at beg. of next 2 rows.
Cast off 2 sts. at beg. of foll. 2 rows.
Dec. 1 st. at both ends of next and foll. 9 right-side rows. [92(96:98:102) sts.]
Cont. straight in patt. until armholes measure 27(27:28:28) cm. (10½(10½:11: 11) in.), ending with a wrong side row.

**Shape Shoulders**
Cast off 10(11:11:11) sts. at beg. of next 4 rows.
Cast off 10(10:10:11) sts. at beg. of foll. 2 rows. [32(32:34:36) sts.]
Change to 3mm. needles.
Work 10 rows in k.1, p.1 rib.
Cast off in rib.

## FRONT

Work as for back until 108(112:114:118) sts. rem. in armhole shaping, ending with a wrong side row.

**Shape Neck**
*1st row:* p.2 tog., patt. 50(52:53:55), p.2 tog., turn and work on these 52(54:55:57) sts.
Leave rem. 54(56:57:59) sts. on a spare needle.
** Work 1 row straight.
Dec. 1 st. at armhole edge on next row.
Work 1 row straight.
Dec. 1 st. at both ends of next row.
Work 1 row straight.
Dec. 1 st. at armhole edge on next row.

46

Work 1 row straight.
Rep. last 4 rows twice. [42(44:45:47) sts.]
Dec. 1 st. at neck edge on next and every foll. 4th row until 30(32:32:33) sts. rem.
Cont. straight until work measures same as back to shoulders, ending at armhole edge.

**Shape Shoulder**
Cast off 10(11:11:11) sts. at beg. of next and foll. alt. row.
Work 1 row straight.
Cast off rem. 10(10:10:11) sts.
With right side of work facing, rejoin yarn to first of rem. 54(56:57:59) sts.
*1st row*: p.2 tog., patt. 50(52:53:55), p.2 tog.
Now work from ** to end as for first side.

## FRONT NECKBAND

With right side facing and 3mm. needles, beg. at left front shoulder, pick up and k.61(61:65:65) sts. down neck edge to centre, pick up and k. 1 st. from centre V, then pick up and k.61(61:65:65) sts. to right front shoulder. [123(123:131:131) sts.]
*1st row*: k.1, * p.1, k.1 * rep. from * to * to centre V, p. centre st., k.1, then rep. from * to * to end.
*2nd row*: p.1, * k.1, p.1 *, rep. from * to * to 2 sts. before centre st., k.2 tog. t.b.l., k. centre st., k.2 tog., p.1, rep. from * to * to end.
*3rd row*: * k.1, p.1 *, rep. from * to * to centre st., p.1, ** p.1, k.1, rep. from ** to end.
*4th row*: * p.1, k.1 *, rep. from * to * to 2 sts. before centre st., p.2 tog. t.b.l., p.2 tog., then rib to end.
Rep. last 4 rows once and 1st row again.
Cast off loosely in rib, dec. as before.

## ARMBANDS

Sew up shoulder seams, carrying seams across neckband.
With right side facing and 3mm. needles, pick up and k.152(152:158:158) sts. around armhole.
Work 9 rows in k.1, p.1 rib.
Cast off loosely in rib.

## MAKING UP

Press work.
Sew up side seams, carrying seams across armbands.

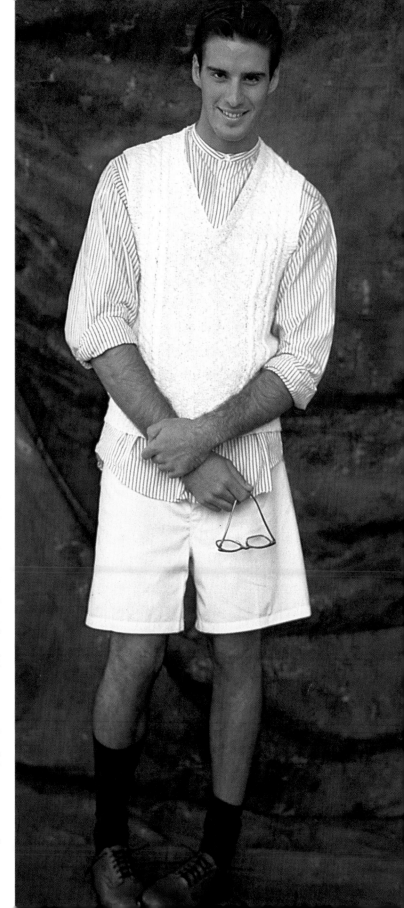

# V-neck, Check-pattern Sweater · 1940

*Loose, V-neck sweater with ribbed welts, set-in sleeves and check pattern on front, back and outside of sleeve*

★★★ Suitable for experienced knitters only

## MATERIALS

**Yarn**
Argyll Ambridge DK
12(12:12:13:13) × 50g. balls

**Needles**
1 pair 3¼mm.
1 pair 4mm.
1 set of 4 double-pointed 3¼mm.

## MEASUREMENTS

**Chest**
92(97:102:107:112) cm.
36(38:40:42:44) in.

**Length**
64(65:66:68:69) cm.
25(25½:26:26¾:27) in.

**Sleeve Seam**
47(47:47:48:48) cm.
18½(18½:18½:18¾:18¾) in.

## TENSION

22 sts. and 30 rows = 10 cm. (4 in.) square over patt. on 4mm. needles. If your tension square does not correspond to these measurements, adjust the needle size used.

## ABBREVIATIONS

k. = knit; p. = purl; st(s). = stitch(es); inc. = increas(ing); dec. = decreas(ing); beg. = begin(ning); rem. = remain(ing); rep. = repeat; alt. = alternate; tog. = together; sl. = slip (transfer one stitch from left needle, knitwise unless otherwise stated, to right hand needle.); cont. = continue; patt. = pattern; foll. = following; folls. = follows; mm. = millimetres; cm. = centimetres; in. = inches; st. st. = stocking st.: one row k., one row p.; g. st. = garter st.: every row k.; incs. = increases; decs. = decreases.

## FRONT

Cast on 101(107:113:119:125) sts. with 3¼mm. needles.
*1st row*: k.2, (p.1, k.1) to last st., k.1.
*2nd row*: k.1, (p.1, k.1) to end.
Rep. these 2 rows for 7 cm. (2¾ in.), ending with a 2nd row and inc. 9 sts.

evenly on last row. [110(116:122:128:134) sts.]
Change to 4mm. needles and work in patt. as folls.:
*1st row (right side)*: k.8(11:14:8:11), (p.4, k.14) to last 12(15:18:12:15) sts., p.4, k.8(11:14:8:11).
*2nd row*: p.8(11:14:8:11), (k.4, p.14) to last 12(15:18:12:15) sts., k.4, p.8(11:14:8:11).
*3rd and 4th rows*: as 1st and 2nd.
*5th row*: k.7(10:13:7:10), (p.1, k.4, p.1, k.12) to last 13(16:19:13:16) sts., p.1, k.4, p.1, k.7(10:13:7:10).
*6th row*: p.6(9:12:6:9), (k.1, p.6, k.1, p.10) to last 14(17:20:14:17) sts., k.1, p.6, k.1, p.6(9:12:6:9).
*7th row*: k.5(8:11:5:8), (p.1, k.8) to last 6(9:12:6:9) sts., p.1, k.5(8:11:5:8).
*8th row*: p.4(7:10:4:7), (k.1, p.10, k.1, p.6) to last 16(19:22:16:19) sts., k.1, p.10, k.1, p.4(7:10:4:7).
*9th row*: k.3(6:9:3:6), (p.1, k.12, p.1, k.4) to last 17(20:23:17:20) sts., p.1, k.12, p.1, k.3(6:9:3:6).
*10th row*: p.1(4:7:1:4), (k.2, p.14, k.2) to last 1(4:7:1:4) sts., p.1(4:7:1:4).
*11th row*: k.1(4:7:1:4), (p.2, k.14, p.2) to last 1(4:7:1:4) sts., k.1(4:7:1:4).
*12th and 13th rows*: as 10th and 11th.
*14th row*: p.3(6:9:3:6), (k.1, p.12, k.1, p.4) to last 17(20:23:17:20) sts., k.1, p.12, k.1, p.3(6:9:3:6).
*15th row*: k.4(7:10:4:7), (p.1, k.10, p.1, k.6) to last 16(19:22:16:19) sts., þ.1, k.10, p.1, k.4(7:10:4:7).
*16th row*: p.5(8:11:5:8), (k.1, p.8) to last 6(9:12:6:9) sts., k.1, p.5(8:11:5:8).

*17th row*: k.6(9:12:6:9), (p.1, k.6, p.1, k.10) to last 14(17:20:14:17) sts., p.1, k.6, p.1, k.6(9:12:6:9).
*18th row*: p.7(10:13:7:10), (k.1, p.4, k.1, p.12) to last 13(16:19:13:16) sts., k.1, p.4, k.1, p.7(10:13:7:10).
These 18 rows form patt.
Cont. in patt. until work measures 41 cm. (16 in.) from beg., ending with a wrong side row.

### Shape Armholes

Keeping patt. correct, cast off 6(7:8:9:10) sts. at beg. of next 2 rows.
Dec. 1 st. at each end of next 7 rows, then on the 4 foll. alt. rows. [76(80:84:88: 92) sts.]

### Shape Neck

*Next row (wrong side)*: patt. 38(40:42:44: 46), turn.
Cont. on these sts.
Dec. 1 st. at neck edge on foll. 3rd row, then on every foll. alt. row until 28(29:31: 33:35) sts. rem., then on every foll. 4th row until 23(24:25:26:27) sts. rem.
Work straight until front measures 23(24:25:27:28) cm. (9(9½:9¾:10½:11) in.) from beg. of armhole shaping, ending at armhole edge.

### Shape Shoulder

Cast off 8(8:8:9:9) sts. at beg. of next and foll. alt. row.
Work 1 row.
Cast off.
With wrong side facing, rejoin yarn to rem. sts. and patt. 1 row.
Complete as first half.

## BACK

Work as for front until armhole shaping is complete.
Work straight until back measures same as front to shoulder shaping, ending with a wrong side row.

### Shape Shoulders

Cast off 8(8:8:9:9) sts. at beg. of next 4 rows.
Cast off 7(8:9:8:9) sts. at beg. of next 2 rows.
Sl. rem. 30(32:34:36:38) sts. onto a spare needle.

## SLEEVES

Cast on 49(51:53:55:57) sts. with 3¼mm. needles.

Work in rib as on welt for 7 cm. (2¾ in.), ending with a 2nd row and inc. 7(5:9: 7:11) sts. evenly across last row. [56(56: 62:62:68) sts.]

Change to 4mm. needles and work patt. as folls.:

1st and 2nd sizes only: work 1st to 4th rows as given for 1st size on front.

3rd and 4th sizes only: work 1st to 4th rows as given for 2nd size on front.

5th size only: work 1st to 4th rows as given for 3rd size on front.

All sizes: cont. in patt. to match front, at the same time shape sleeve by inc. 1 st. at each end of next row, then on every foll. 6th(4th:4th:4th:4th) row until there are 78(62:68:76:82) sts., then on every foll. 8th(6th:6th:6th:6th) row until there are 88(92:98:102:108) sts., taking extra sts. into st. st.

Work straight until sleeve measures 47(47:47:48:48) cm. (18½(18½:18½:18¾: 18¾) in.) from beg., ending with a wrong side row.

### Shape Top

Cast off 6(7:8:9:10) sts. at beg. of next 2 rows.

Dec. 1 st. at each end of every right side row until 44 sts. rem., then on every row until 34 sts. rem.

Cast off.

### NECKBAND

Sew up shoulder seams.

With set of 3¼mm. needles and right side facing, k. across sts. of back, k. up 44(47:50:53:56) sts. evenly down left front neck, pick up and k. into back of horizontal thread lying between the 2 centre sts., finally k. up 43(46:49:52:55) sts. evenly up right front neck. [118(126:134: 142:150) sts.]

Keeping centre st. as a k. st. on every round, work 9 rounds in k.1, p.1 rib, dec. 1 st. at each side of centre st. on every round.

Cast off in rib.

### MAKING UP

Omitting ribbing, press lightly.
Sew up side and sleeve seams.
Set in sleeves.
Press seams.

---

# Cross-neck Sweater

*Long, thick, stocking-stitch sweater with set-in sleeves, ribbed hem, cuff and crossover neck welts*

★ Suitable for beginners

## MATERIALS

### Yarn
Chat Botté Petrouchka
10(11:11:12:12:13:13) × 50g. balls

### Needles
1 pair 2¾mm.
1 pair 3¾mm.

## MEASUREMENTS

### Bust/Chest
82(87:92:97:102:107:112) cm.
32(34:36:38:40:42:44) in.

### Length
61(62:63:64:65:66:67) cm.
24(24¼:24¾:25:25½:26:26¼) in.

### Sleeve Seam
43(44:45:46:47:48:49) cm.
16¾(17¼:17¾:18:18½:18¾:19¼) in.

## TENSION

24 sts. and 32 rows = 10 cm. (4 in.) square over st.st. on 3¾mm. needles. If your tension square does not correspond to these measurements, adjust the needle size used.

## ABBREVIATIONS

k.=knit; p.=purl; st(s).=stitch(es); inc.= increase; dec.=decrease; beg.=begin(ning); rem. = remain(ing); rep. = repeat; alt. = alternate; tog. = together; sl. = slip stitch (transfer one stitch from left needle, knitwise unless otherwise stated, to right hand needle.); cont. = continue; patt. = pattern; foll. = following; folls. = follows; mm. = millimetres; cm. = centimetres; in. = inch(es); st.st. = stocking stitch.

## BACK

Cast on 109(115:121:127:133:139:145) sts. with 2¾mm. needles.
*1st row:* k.1, * p.1, k.1, rep. from * to end.
*2nd row:* p.1, * k.1, p.1, rep. from * to end.
Rep 1st and 2nd row for 8 cm. (3¼ in.), ending with 2nd row.
Change to 3¾mm. needles.
Cont. in st.st., starting with a k. row.
Work until back measures 42 cm. (16½ in.) ending with a p. row.

## Shape Armholes

Cast off 5(5:6:6:7:7:8) sts. at beg. of next 2 rows.

Cast off 2 sts. at beg. of next 4 rows.

Dec. 1 st. at each end of next and foll. 3(4:4:5:5:6:6) alt. rows. [85(89:93:97:101:105:109) sts.]

Cont. straight until armholes measure 19(20:21:22:23:24:25) cm. (7½(7¾:8¼:8½:9:9½:9¾) in.), ending with a p. row.

## Shape Shoulders

Cast off 4(5:5:5:6:6:6) sts. at beg. of next 8 rows.

Cast off 7(4:6:7:5:6:7) sts. at beg. of next 2 rows.

Cast off rem. 39(41:41:43:43:45:47) sts.

## FRONT

Work as back until end of armhole shaping, ending with a p. row.

Work 2 more rows.

### Shape Neckline

*Next row:* k.37(39:40:42:43:45:47), cast off 11(11:13:13:15:15:15), k. to end.

P. last group of sts. and place rem. sts. on spare needle.

Working only with sts. just purled, dec. 1 st. at neck edge on every alt. row 14(15:14:15:14:15:16) times. [23(24:26:27:29:30:31) sts.]

Cont. straight until armhole measures the same as on back, ending with a k. row.

### Shape Shoulder

Cast off 4(5:5:5:6:6:6) sts. at beg. of next and foll. 3 alt. rows.

*Next row:* k.

Cast off rem. 7(4:6:7:5:6:7) sts.

Return to sts. on spare needle and work to match 1st side, reversing all shapings.

## SLEEVES

Cast on 65(67:69:71:73:75:77) sts. with 2¾mm. needles.

Work in k.1, p.1 rib as on back for 8 cm. (3¼ in.), ending with 2nd row.

Change to 3¾mm. needles.

Cont. in st.st.

AT THE SAME TIME, inc. 1 st. at each end of next and foll. 8th row 13(13:14:14:15:15:15) times. [91(93:97:99:103:105:107) sts.]

Cont. straight until sleeve measures 43(44:45:46:47:48:49) cm. (16¾(17¼:17¾:18:18½:18¾:19¼) in.), ending with a p. row.

### Shape Top

Cast off 5(5:6:6:7:7:8) sts. at beg. of next 2 rows.

Cast off 2 sts. at beg. of next 4 rows.

Dec. 1 st. at each end of next and foll. 8(9:10:11:12:13:13) alt. rows. [55 sts.]

*Next row:* p.

Cast off 2 sts. at beg. of next 4 rows.

Cast off 3 sts. at beg. of foll. 4 rows.

Cast off 4 sts. at beg. of foll. 4 rows.

Cast off rem. 19 sts.

## COLLAR

Cast on 251(257:261:267:271:277:281) sts. with 2¾mm. needles.

Work in k.1, p.1 rib as on back for 5(5:6:6:7:7:7) cm. (2(2:2¼:2¼:2¾:2¾:2¾) in.).

Always in rib, cast off 4 sts. at beg. of next 8 rows.

Cast off 5 sts. at beg. of foll. 6 rows.

Cast off 6 sts. at beg. of foll. 20 rows.

Cast off 8 sts. at beg. of foll. 4 rows.

Cast off 6(7:9:10:12:13:15) sts. at beg. of foll. 2 rows.

Cast off rem. 25(29:29:33:33:37:37) sts.

## MAKING UP

Do not press. Sew up shoulder seams.

Sew up side and sleeve seams.

Set in sleeves.

Sew up shaped edge of collar to neck edge, fixing the straight edge to cast off sts. at centre front so that they overlap right over left for woman and left over right for man.

# Knitted Shirt-style Sweater 1934

*Stretchy-rib, long sweater with set-in sleeves, buttoned front placket, patterned collar and ribbed welts*

★★ Suitable for knitters with some previous experience

## MATERIALS

### Yarn
Sirdar Countrystyle 4 ply
10(11:11:12) × 50g. balls

### Needles
1 pair 2¾mm.
1 pair 3¼mm.

### Buttons
3

## MEASUREMENTS

### Chest
92(97:102:107) cm.
36(38:40:42) in.

### Length
65(66:67:68) cm.
25½(26:26¼:26¾) in.

### Sleeve Seam
48 cm.
18¾ in.

## TENSION
30 sts. and 36 rows = 10 cm. (4 in.) square over patt. on 3¼mm. needles. If your tension square does not correspond to these measurements, adjust the needle size used.

## ABBREVIATIONS
k.=knit; p.=purl; st(s).=stitch(es); inc.= increase; dec.=decrease; beg.=begin(ning); rem. = remain(ing); rep. = repeat; alt. = alternate; tog. = together; sl. = slip stitch (transfer one stitch from left needle, knitwise unless otherwise stated, to right hand needle.); cont. = continue; patt.= pattern; foll. = following; folls. = follows; mm. = millimetres; cm. = centimetres; in. = inch(es); st.st. = stocking stitch; y.r.n. = yarn round needle.

## BACK
Cast on 146(154:162:170) sts. with 2¾mm. needles.
*1st row:* k.2, * p.2, k.2, rep. from * to end.
*2nd row:* p.2, * k.2, p.2, rep. from * to end.
Rep. 1st and 2nd row for 5 cm. (2 in.) ending with 2nd row. Change to 3¼mm. needles and work in patt.:
*1st row:* k.2, * y.r.n., k.2, pass the y.r.n. over the 2 sts. just worked, k.2, rep. from * to end.
*2nd row:* p.2, * k.2, p.2, rep. from * to end.

These 2 rows form the patt.
Cont. in patt. until work measures 44 cm. (17¼ in.), ending with a 2nd row.

### Shape Armholes
Keeping patt. correct, cast off 6 sts. at beg. of next 2 rows.
Cast off 2 sts. at beg. of next 4 rows.
Dec. 1 st. at each end of next and foll. 3(5:7:9) alt. rows. [118(122:126:130) sts.]
Cont. straight until armholes measure 21(22:23:24) cm. (8¼(8½:9:9½) in.), ending with a 2nd row.

### Shape Shoulders
Cast off 8(8:8:8) sts. at beg. of next 4 rows.
Cast off 8(8:8:9) sts. at beg. of next 2 rows.
Cast off 8(8:9:9) sts. at beg. of next 2 rows.
Cast off 8(9:9:9) sts. at beg. of next 2 rows.
Cast off rem. 38(40:42:44) sts.

## FRONT
Work as back to 1 row less than needed for armholes.

### Divide for Front Opening
*Next row* (wrong side): patt. 70(74:78:82) sts., cast off 6, patt. to end.
Cont. on last 70(74:78:82) sts., leaving rem. sts. on spare needle.

### Shape Armhole
Cast off 6 sts. at beg. of next row.
Cast off 2 sts. at beg. of foll. 2 alt. rows.
Dec. 1 st. at beg. of foll. 4(6:8:10) alt. rows. [56(58:60:62) sts.]
Cont. straight until armhole measures 14(14:15:15) cm. (5½(5½:5¾:5¾) in.,) ending with 1st row.

### Shape Neck and Shoulder
Cast off 6(7:8:9) sts. at beg. of next row.
Cast off 4 sts. at beg. of foll. alt. row.
Cast off 2 sts. at beg. of foll. 2 alt. rows.
Dec. 1 st. at beg. of foll. 2 alt. rows. [40(41:42:43) sts.]
Cont. straight until armhole measures the same as on back, ending with 2nd row.
Cast off shoulder as on back.
Return to sts. on spare needle.
Rejoin yarn and work as for left front, reversing all shapings.

## SLEEVES
Cast on 66(70:70:74) sts. with 2¾mm. needles.
Work in k.2, p.2 rib as on back for 8 cm. (3¼ in.) ending with 2nd row.
Change to 3¼mm. needles.
Cont. in patt. as on back.
AT THE SAME TIME, inc. 1 st. at each end of 1st and every foll. 4th row until there are 110(114:118:122) sts.

Cont. straight until sleeve measures 48 cm. (18¾ in.) or required length, ending with 2nd row.

### Shape Top
Cast off 6 sts. at beg. of next 2 rows.
Dec. 1 st. at each end of next and foll. 15 alt. rows, ending with a 2nd row.
Cast off 2 sts. at beg. of next 16(18:20:22) rows.
Cast off 3 sts. at beg. of next 4 rows.
Cast off 4 sts. at beg. of next 2 rows.
Cast off rem. 14 sts.

## FRONT BANDS
With 2¾mm. needles and right side facing, pick up 44(44:48:48) sts. evenly along right front edge of opening.
*1st row* (wrong side): k.1, * p.2, k.2, rep. from * to last 3 sts., p.2, k.1.
*2nd row:* k.3, * p.2, k.2, rep. from * to last st., k.1.
Work 1st and 2nd row 3 more times.
Cast off in rib.
Pick up sts. from left edge and work as for right band for 3 rows.
*4th row:* rib 3, (cast off 2, rib 14) twice, cast off 2, rib 7(7:11:11).
*5th row:* rib to end, casting on 2 sts. over each 2 cast off.
Rib 3 more rows. Cast off in rib.

## COLLAR
Cast on 38(38:42:42) sts. with 3¼mm. needles.
Work in patt. as on back.
AT THE SAME TIME, cast on 4 sts. at beg. of 2nd and foll. 11 rows.
Cast on 8(8:10:10) sts. at beg. of next 2 rows, ending with 1st row. [102(102: 108:108) sts.]
*Next row:* k.2, patt. to last 2 sts., k.2.
Cont. in patt., keeping 2 sts. at each end in garter st., for 4 rows.
*Next row:* k.2, inc. 1 by picking up loop between sts. and k. into the back of it, patt. to last 2 sts., inc. 1, k.2.
Cont. inc. on every 4th row until side edge measures 7(7:8:8) cm. (2¾(2¾:3¼:3¼) in.), ending with 2nd row.
Cast off loosely in patt.

## MAKING UP
Press work, if required, following instructions on ball band.
Sew up shoulder seams. Set in sleeves.
Sew up side and sleeve seams.
Sew up lower edges of front bands.
Sew on collar, starting and ending in centre of front bands.
Press seams if required. Sew on buttons.

# Shetland Sports Sweater

*1950*

*Lightweight yet warm shetland sweater in easy, textured pattern, with set-in sleeves, ribbed welts and narrow roll-collar*

★ Suitable for beginners

## MATERIALS

**Yarn**
Pingouin Pingolaine
8(9:9:10) × 50g. balls

**Needles**
1 pair 3mm.
1 pair 3¾mm.
1 set of 4 double-pointed 3mm.
1 cable needle

## MEASUREMENTS

**Chest**
95(100:105:110) cm.
37½(39½:41½:43½) in.

**Length**
66(68:70:72) cm.
26(26¾:27½:28¼) in.

**Sleeve Seam**
48(49:50:51) cm.
18¾(19¼:19½:20) in.

## TENSION

27 sts. = 10 cm. (4 in.) over patt. on 3¾mm. needles. If your tension does not correspond to these measurements, adjust the needle size used.

## ABBREVIATIONS

k.=knit; p.=purl; st(s).=stitch(es); inc.= increase; dec.=decrease; beg.=begin(ning); rem. = remain(ing); rep. = repeat; alt. = alternate; tog. = together; sl. = slip stitch (transfer one stitch from left needle, knit-wise unless otherwise stated, to right hand needle.); cont. = continue; patt. = pattern; foll. = following; folls. = follows; mm. = millimetres; cm. = centimetres; in. = inch(es); st.st. = stocking stitch; c.4 = cable 4: sl. next 2 sts. onto cable needle, hold at back of work, k. next 2 sts., k.2 sts. from cable needle.

## BACK

Cast on 130(138:146:154) sts. with 3mm. needles.
Work in k.2, p.2 rib for 8 cm. (3¼ in.), inc. 10 sts. evenly across last row. [140(148:156:164) sts.]
Change to 3¾mm. needles and patt.:
*1st row:* p.4, * k.4, p.4, rep. from * to end.
*2nd row:* k.4, * p.4, k.4, rep. from * to end.
*3rd row:* p.4, * c.4, p.4, rep. from * to end.
*4th row:* as 2nd.
*5th row:* as 2nd.

*6th row:* as 1st.
*7th row:* c.4, * p.4, c.4, rep. from * to end.
*8th row:* as 1st.
These 8 rows form the patt. and are rep. throughout.
Cont. in patt. until work measures 45(46:47:48) cm. 17¾(18:18½:18¾ in.), ending with a wrong side row.

### Shape Armholes
Cast off 8 sts. at beg. of next 2 rows.
Dec. 1 st. at each end of next and every alt. row until there are 108(116:124:132) sts.
Work without shaping until armholes measure 21(22:23:24) cm. (8¼(8½:9:9½) in.), ending with a wrong side row.

### Shape Shoulders
Cast off 11(12:13:14) sts. at beg. of next 6 rows.
Sl. rem. 42(44:46:48) sts. onto holder.

## FRONT

Work as for back until armholes measure

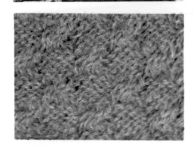

13(14:15:16) cm. (5(5½:5¾:6¼) in.), ending with a wrong side row.

### Shape Neck
Patt. across 67(72:77:82) sts. and place these on holder, patt. across rem. 41(44:47:50) sts. for 1st side of neck and shoulder.
Dec. 1 st. at neck edge on next and every row until there are 33(36:39:42) sts.
Cont. in patt. until armhole measures same as back to shoulder, ending at arm-hole edge.

### Shape Shoulder
Cast off 11(12:13:14) sts. at beg. of next and foll. 2 alt. rows.
Leave centre 26(28:30:32) sts. on holder, rejoin yarn at centre front and work 2nd side to correspond with 1st side, reversing shaping.

## SLEEVES

Cast on 64(64:72:72) sts. with 3mm. needles.
Work in k.2, p.2 rib for 8 cm. (3¼ in.), inc. 4 sts. evenly across last row. [68(68:76:76) sts.]
Change to 3¾mm. needles and patt. as given for back, inc. 1 st. at each end of 5th and every foll. 6th row until there are 100(104:108:112) sts.
Work without shaping until sleeve measures 48(49:50:51) cm. (18¾(19¼:19½:20) in.).

### Shape Top
Cast off 8 sts. at beg. of next 2 rows.
Keeping patt. correct, dec. 1 st. at each end of next and every alt. row until 44 sts. rem.
Cast off 2 sts. at beg. of next 6 rows.
Cast off rem. 32 sts.

## NECKBAND

Sew up shoulder seams.
With right side of work facing, and using set of 3mm. needles, pick up and k.40 sts. down left side of neck, k. across 26(28:30:32) sts. from centre front, pick up and k.40 sts. up right side of neck and k. across rem. 42(44:46:48) sts. from back. [148(152:156:160) sts.]
Work in k.2, p.2 rib for 8 cm. (3¼ in.).
Cast off loosely, in rib.

## MAKING UP

Set in sleeves, matching centre of sleeve head to shoulder seam.
Sew up side and sleeve seams.
Press, using damp cloth and warm iron.

# Banded Ski Sweater

*Thick, unisex sweater in ribbed and two-tone stocking-stitch pattern bands, with set-in sleeves, ribbed polo neck and welts*

★★ Suitable for knitters with some previous experience

## MATERIALS

**Yarn**
Sirdar Countrystyle DK
6(7:8:9) × 50g. balls (Main Col. A)
3(4:5:5) × 50g. balls (Contrast Col. B)

**Needles**
1 pair 3¼mm.
1 pair 4mm.

## MEASUREMENTS

**Chest**
92(97:102:107) cm.
36(38:40:42) in.

**Length**
64(65:66:67) cm.
25(25½:26:26¼) in.

**Sleeve Seam**
49 cm.
19¼ in.

## TENSION

22 sts. = 10 cm. (4 in.) over 2-colour patt. on 4mm. needles. If your tension does not correspond to these measurements, adjust the needle size used.

## ABBREVIATIONS

k.=knit; p.=purl; st(s).=stitch(es); inc.= increase; dec.=decrease; beg.=begin(ning); rem. = remain(ing); rep. = repeat; alt. = alternate; tog. = together; sl. = slip stitch (transfer one stitch from left needle, knitwise unless otherwise stated, to right hand needle.); cont. = continue; patt. = pattern; foll. = following; folls. = follows; mm. = millimetres; cm. = centimetres; in. = inch(es); st.st. = stocking stitch; m.1 = make 1 st.: pick up horizontal loop lying before next st. and work into back of it.

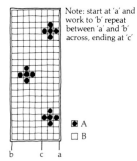

Note: start at 'a' and work to 'b' repeat between 'a' and 'b' across, ending at 'c'

■ A
□ B

b    c    a

## BACK

Cast on 103(109:115:121) sts. with 3¼mm. needles and A.
*1st row:* k.1, * p.1, k.1, rep. from * to end.
*2nd row:* p.1, * k.1, p.1, rep. from * to end.
Rep. 1st and 2nd rows for 8 cm. (3¼ in.) ending with 1st row.
*Next row:* rib 6(9:12:15), m.1, (rib 13, m.1) 7 times, rib 6(9:12:15).
[111(117:123:129) sts.]
Change to 4mm. needles.
** Joining in and breaking off colours as required, work in st.st., foll. patt. from chart and leaving 2(1:0:3) sts. at each end without patt. [21 rows in 2 colours.]
*Next row* (wrong side): with A, p.
*Next row:* with A, k.1, * p.1, k.1, rep. from * to end.
Rep. these 2 rows 10 more times.
Joining in B, work 2-colour patt. starting on the wrong side with a p. row.
*Next row:* with A, k.
*Next row:* with A, p.1, * k.1, p.1, rep. from * to end.
Rep. these 2 rows 10 more times.
Rep. from ** for as long as required.
AT THE SAME TIME, when work measures 41 cm. (16 in.), shape armholes.

**Shape Armholes**
Cast off 5(6:7:8) sts. at beg. of next 2 rows.
Dec. 1 st. at both ends of next and foll. 6(7:7:8) alt. rows. [85(89:93:95) sts.]
Work straight until armhole measures 23(24:25:26) cm. (9(9½:9¾:10½) in.)

**Shape Shoulders**
Cast off 7 sts. at beg. of next 6 rows.
Cast off 6(8:7:8) sts. at beg. of next 2 rows.
Leave rem. 33(35:37:39) sts. on holder.

## FRONT

Work as back to 7 cm. (2¾ in.) below top of centre back.

**Shape Neck and Shoulders**
Patt. 36(38:37:38) sts.

Leave rem. sts. on spare needle, turn.
Dec. 4 sts. at beg. of next row.
Dec. 2 sts. at neck edge on foll. alt. row.
Dec. 1 st. at neck edge 3 times on foll. alt rows.
Cont. straight to same row as back for shoulder shaping.

**Shape Shoulder**
Work as for back.
Return to sts. on spare needle.
Sl. 15(17:19:21) sts. onto holder.
Rejoin yarn and work as for left side, reversing all shapings.

## SLEEVES

Cast on 53(55:57:59) sts. with 3¼mm. needles and A.
Work in k.1, p.1 rib for 8 cm. (3¼ in.)
Change to 4mm. needles.
*1st row:* k.1, * p.1, k.1, rep. from * to end.
*2nd row:* p.
Rep. these 2 rows 10 more times.
Cont. in patt. as on back from ** to **, rep. as required.
AT THE SAME TIME, inc. 1 st. at each end of 3rd row and every foll. 6th row to obtain 79(81:75:77) sts.
Inc. 1 st. at each end of every foll. 5th row to obtain 87(89:93:95) sts.
Cont. straight until work measures approx. 49 cm. (19¼ in.), ending with same row as back at underarm.

**Shape Top**
Cast off 5(6:7:8) sts. at beg. of next 2 rows.
Dec. 1 st. at each end of next and every foll. alt. row to obtain 39(37:37:33) sts.
Work 1 row.
Cast off 4 sts. at beg. of next 6 rows.
Cast off rem. 15(13:13:9) sts.

## POLO COLLAR

Sew up left shoulder seam.
With right side facing, 3¼mm. needles and A, k. up half the sts. on back holder, m.1, k. up rem. sts. on holder, pick up 35 sts. down left front neck, k. up 15(17:19:21) sts. on front holder, pick up 35 sts. up right front neck. [119(123:127:131) sts.]
Work in p.1, k.1 rib for 16 cm. (6¼ in.)
Cast off loosely.

## MAKING UP

Press each piece lightly following instructions on ball band.
Sew up right shoulder seam and polo-neck seam.
Sew up side and sleeve seams.
Set in sleeves. Press seams if required.

# Slash-neck Sweater with Giant Cable 1956

*Loose sweater with garter-striped body, ribbed sleeves, centre-front cable and slash neck with facing*

★★ Suitable for knitters with some previous experience

## MATERIALS

**Yarn**
Argyll Pure Wool Aran
16(17:17:18:18) × 50g. balls

**Needles**
1 pair 3¾mm.
1 pair 4½mm.
1 cable needle

## MEASUREMENTS

**Chest**
92(97:102:107:112) cm.
36(38:40:42:44) in.

**Length**
65(66:68:69:70) cm.
25½(26:26¾:27:27½) in.

**Sleeve Seam**
46(47:47:47:48) cm.
18(18½:18½:18½:18¾) in.

## TENSION

18 sts. and 24 rows = 10 cm. (4 in.) square over st. st. on 4½mm. needles. If your tension square does not correspond to these measurements, adjust the needle size used.

## ABBREVIATIONS

k.=knit; p.=purl; st(s).=stitch(es); inc.= increas(ing); dec.=decreas(ing); beg.= begin(ning); rem. = remain(ing); rep. = repeat; alt. = alternate; tog. = together; sl. = slip (transfer one stitch from left needle, knitwise unless otherwise stated, to right hand needle.); cont. = continue; patt. = pattern; foll. = following; folls. = follows; mm. = millimetres; cm. = centimetres; in. = inches; st. st. = stocking st.: one row k., one row p.; g. st. = garter st.: every row k.; incs. = increases; decs. = decreases; C8 = cable 8: sl. next 4 sts. onto cable needle and leave at back of work, k.4, k.4 from cable needle.

## BACK

Cast on 84(88:92:96:100) sts. with 3¾mm. needles.
*1st row:* k.3, (p.2, k.2) to last st., k.1.
*2nd row:* k.1, (p.2, k.2) to last 3 sts., p.2, k.1.
Rep. these 2 rows for 7 cm. (2¾ in.), ending with a 2nd row and inc. 6 sts. evenly on last row. [90(94:98:102:106) sts.]

Change to 4½mm. needles and patt. as folls.:
*1st row (right side):* p.
*2nd and 3rd rows:* k.
*4th row:* p.
These 4 rows form patt.
Cont. in patt. until work measures 44 cm. (17¼ in.) at centre, ending with a wrong side row.

### Shape Armholes

Keeping patt. correct, cast off 5(6:7:8:9) sts. at beg. of next 2 rows.
Dec. 1 st. at each end of next 5 rows, then at each end of the 3 foll. alt. rows. [64(66:68:70:72) sts.]
Work straight until back measures 20(21:23:24:25) cm. (7¾(8¼:9:9½:9¾) in.) from beg. of armhole shaping, ending with a wrong side row.

### Shape Shoulders

Cast off 5(5:6:6:6) sts. at beg. of next 4 rows.
Cast off 6(6:5:5:6) sts. at beg. of next 2 rows.

### Shape Neck Facing

Beg. with a k. row, work 4 rows in st. st.
Cast off 2 sts. at beg. of next 6 rows.
Cast off loosely.

## FRONT

Work ribbing as for back, but inc. 12 sts. evenly on last row. [96(100:104:108:112) sts.]
Change to 4½mm. needles.
Work in patt. with centre cable as folls.:

*1st row (right side):* p.40(42:44:46:48), k.2, p.2, C8, p.2, k.2, p.40(42:44:46:48).
*2nd row:* k.40(42:44:46:48), p.2, k.2, p.8, k.2, p.2, k.40(42:44:46:48).
*3rd row:* k.42(44:46:48:50), p.2, k.8, p.2, k. to end.
*4th row:* p.42(44:46:48:50), k.2, p.8, k.2, p. to end.
*5th row:* p.40(42:44:46:48), k.2, p.2, k.8, p.2, k.2, p.40(42:44:46:48).
*6th to 8th rows:* as 2nd to 4th.
*9th to 12th rows:* as 5th to 8th.
These 12 rows form patt.
Cont. in patt. until front measures same as back to armhole shaping, ending with a wrong side row.

### Shape Armholes

Work as for back. [70(72:74:76:78) sts.]
Work straight until front measures same as back to shoulder shaping, ending with a wrong side row.
Shape shoulders as for back.

### Shape Neck Facing

Beg. with a k. row, work 4 rows in st. st., dec. 3 sts. evenly over centre 12 sts. on 1st row.
Cast off 2 sts. at beg. of next 6 rows.
Cast off loosely.

## SLEEVES

Cast on 40(40:44:44:48) sts. with 3¾mm. needles.
Work in rib as on welt for 7 cm. (2¾ in.).
Change to 4½mm. needles.
Cont. in rib, shaping sleeve by inc. 1 st. at each end of next row, then on every foll. 6th(4th:4th:3rd:3rd) row until there are 50(52:56:62:58) sts., then on every foll 4th row until there are 78(82:86:90:94) sts., taking extra sts. into rib.
Work straight until sleeve measures 46(47:47:47:48) cm. (18(18½:18½:18½:18¾) in.), ending with a wrong side row.

### Shape Top

Cast off 5(6:7:8:9) sts. at beg. of next 2 rows.
Work 2(4:6:8:10) rows straight.
Dec. 1 st. at each end of next and every foll. alt. row until 46 sts. rem., then on every row until 36 sts. rem.
Cast off.

## MAKING UP

Press lightly, omitting welt and cuffs.
Sew up shoulder seams.
Sew up side and sleeve seams.
Set in sleeves.
Fold facings to wrong side and slip st. in position.
Press seams.

# Ridge-pattern Cardigan

1953

*Rugged, hip-length sports cardigan buttoning to a V neckline, with set-in sleeves, ribbed welts and borders*

★★ Suitable for knitters with some previous experience

## MATERIALS

**Yarn**
Sunbeam St Ives 4 ply
21(21:22:23:23) × 25g. balls.

**Needles**
1 pair 3mm.
1 pair 3¾mm.

**Buttons**
5

## MEASUREMENTS

**Chest**
92(97:102:107:112) cm.
36(38:40:42:44) in.

**Length**
64(66:68:70:71) cm.
25(26:26¾:27½:27¾) in.

**Sleeve Seam**
52(53:55:55:56) cm.
20½(20¾:21½:21½:22) in.

## TENSION

28 sts. and 36 rows = 10 cm. (4 in.) square over patt. slightly stretched on 3¾mm. needles. If your tension square does not correspond to these measurements, adjust the needle size used.

## ABBREVIATIONS

k. = knit; p. = purl; st(s). = stitch(es); inc. = increas(ing); dec. = decreas(ing); beg. = begin(ning); rem. = remain(ing); rep. = repeat; alt. = alternate; tog. = together; sl. = slip (transfer one stitch from left needle, knitwise unless otherwise stated, to right hand needle.); cont. = continue; patt. = pattern; foll. = following; folls. = follows; mm. = millimetres; cm. = centimetres; in. = inches; st. st. = stocking st.: one row k., one row p.; g. st. = garter st.: every row k.; incs. = increases; decs. = decreases.

## BACK

Cast on 155(161:170:176:182) sts. with 3mm. needles.
Work 9 cm. (3½ in.) in rib as folls., ending with a 2nd patt. row:
*1st row (right side):* * k.2, p.1, rep. from * to last 2 sts., k.2.

*2nd row:* * p.2, k.1, rep. from * to last 2 sts., p.2.
*Next row:* inc. 1(2:0:1:2) sts. across the row. [156(163:170:177:184) sts.]
Change to 3¾mm. needles and work as folls.:
*1st row (wrong side):* * k.2, p.5, rep. from * to last 2 sts., k.2.
*2nd row:* ** p.2, k.1, * k.2 tog., then k. again into first st. before slipping sts. off needle, rep. from * once more, rep. from ** to last 2 sts., p.2.
These 2 rows form patt.
Rep. 1st and 2nd rows until back measures 43(44:46:47:48) cm. (16¾(17¼: 18:18½:18¾) in.).

### Shape Armholes

Cast off 6(7:8:9:10) sts. at beg. of next 2 rows.
Dec. 1 st. at each end of every alt. row until 126(131:134:137:140) sts. rem.
Work until armholes measure 21(22:22: 23:23) cm. (8¼(8½:8½:9:9) in.) measured on the straight.

### Shape Shoulders

Cast off at beg. of next and foll. rows 12(12:10:10:11) sts. twice and 10(10:11:11: 11) sts. 6 times.
Cast off rem. sts.

## LEFT FRONT

Cast on 74(77:83:89:92) sts. with 3mm. needles.
Work 9 cm. (3½ in.) in rib as for back ending with 2nd patt. row.
*Next row:* inc. 5(2:3:4:1) sts. evenly across the row. [79(79:86:93:93) sts.]
Change to 3¾mm. needles and work in patt. as for back until front measures same as back to armholes, ending with right side facing.

### Shape Armhole and Neck

*1st row:* cast off 7(7:9:9:10) sts., work to last 2 sts., k.2 tog.
Dec. 1 st. at armhole edge on every alt. row 8(9:9:11:11) times, at the same time dec. at neck edge on every 3rd row until 45(48:46:56:55) sts. rem.
Now dec. at neck edge on every 4th(4th: 2nd:2nd:2nd) row until 42(42:43:43:44) sts. rem.
Work until armhole measures same as back.

### Shape Shoulder

Cast off at armhole edge 12(12:10:10:11) sts. once and 10(10:11:11:11) sts. 3 times.

## RIGHT FRONT

Work as for left front, reversing all shapings.

## SLEEVES

Cast on 77(77:80:83:86) sts. with 3mm. needles.

Work 9 cm. (3½ in.) in rib as for back, ending with a 2nd patt. row.
*Next row:* inc. 2(2:6:3:0) sts. across the row. [79(79:86:86:86) sts.]
Change to 3¾mm. needles and work in patt. as back.
Inc. 1 st. at each end of every 6th row, working all inc. sts. into patt., until there are 119(123:128:132:136) sts.
Work until sleeve measures 52(53:55:55: 56) cm. (20½(20¾:21½:21½:22) in.)

### Shape Top

Cast off 7(8:9:10:11) sts. at beg. of next 2 rows.
Dec. 1 st. at each end of every alt. row 12 times.
Cast off 5 sts. at beg. of next 12 rows.
Cast off rem. sts.

## FRONT BORDER

Cast on 17 sts. with 3mm. needles, and work in rib as given for back.
Work 2 cm. (¾ in.)
Make buttonhole as folls.:
*Next row (right side)*: rib 6 sts., cast off 6 sts., rib to end.
*Next row*: cast on 6 sts. above cast-off sts. of preceding row.
Work 4 more buttonholes 9(9:9:10:10) cm. (3½(3½:3½:4:4) in.) apart.
Work until border is same length as fronts and back neck when slightly stretched.
Cast off.

## MAKING UP

Sew up shoulder seams.
Set in sleeves.
Sew up side and sleeve seams.
Sew up front border to fronts and back neck with buttonholes on left side.
Sew on buttons.
Press lightly.

# Cricket Sweater in Basket Pattern 1937

*Patterned, V-neck cricket sweater in extra-soft yarn, with ribbed hem and cuff welts, garter-stitch neck border*

★★ Suitable for knitters with some previous experience

## MATERIALS

**Yarn**
Jaeger Luxury Spun DK
13(13:14) × 50g. balls

**Needles**
1 pair 3¼mm.
1 pair 4mm.

## MEASUREMENTS

**Bust/Chest**
87(97:107) cm.
34(38:42) in.

**Length**
53(55:56) cm.
20¾(21½:22) in.

**Sleeve Seam**
46(47:48) cm.
18(18½:18¾) in.

## TENSION

26 sts. and 32 rows = 10 cm. (4 in.) square over patt. with 4mm. needles. If your tension square does not correspond to these measurements, adjust the needle size used.

## ABBREVIATIONS

k.=knit; p.=purl; st(s).=stitch(es); inc.= increase; dec.=decrease; beg.=begin(ning); rem. = remain(ing); rep. = repeat; alt. = alternate; tog. = together; sl. = slip stitch (transfer one stitch from left needle, knitwise unless otherwise stated, to right hand needle.); cont. = continue; patt. = pattern; foll. = following; folls. = follows; mm. = millimetres; cm. = centimetres; in. = inch(es); st.st. = stocking stitch; m.1 = make 1 st.: pick up loop from between needles and work into the back of it.

## BACK

Cast on 106(118:130) sts. with 3¼mm. needles.
*1st row*: k.2, * p.2, k.2, rep. from * to end.
*2nd row*: p.2, * k.2, p.2, rep. from * to end.
Rep. 1st and 2nd row for 6 cm. (2¼ in.) ending with a 1st row.
*Next row*: inc. 1 st. at each end of row. [108(120:132) sts.]
AT THE SAME TIME, make a loop with contrasting yarn and place between 54th and 55th (60th and 61st/66th and 67th) sts. to mark centre of work.

Change to 4mm. needles and work as folls.:

87(107) cm. (34(42) in.) sizes only:

*1st row* (right side): p.6, (k.6, p.6) 4(5) times, (p.6, k.6) 4(5) times, p.6.
*2nd and every alt. row:* k. all k. sts. and p. all p. sts.
*3rd row:* as 1st row.
*5th row:* as 1st row.
*7th row:* p.1, m.1, p.2, (k.6, p.6) 8(10) times, k.6, p.2, m.1, p.1. [110(134) sts.]
*9th row:* p.4, (k.6, p.6) 8(10) times, k.6, p.4.
*11th row:* as 9th row.
*13th row:* p.1, m.1, (k.6, p.6) 4(5) times, k.12, (p.6, k.6) 4(5) times, m.1, p.1. [112(136) sts.]
*15th row:* p.2, (k.6, p.6) 4(5) times, k.12, (p.6, k.6) 4(5) times, p.2.
*17th row:* as 15th row.
*19th row:* k.1, m.1, k.4, (p.6, k.6) 8(10) times, p.6, k.4, m.1, k.1. [114(138) sts.]
*21st row:* k.6, (p.6, k.6) 9(11) times.
*23rd row:* as 21st row.
*24th row:* k. all k. sts. and p. all p. sts.
These 24 rows set the patt.

97cm. (38 in.) size only:

*1st row* (right side): (k.6, p.6) 5 times, (p.6, k.6) 5 times.
*2nd and every alt. row:* k. all k. sts. and p. all p. sts.
*3rd row:* as 1st row.
*5th row:* as 1st row.
*7th row:* k.1, m.1, k.2, (p.6, k.6) 9 times, p.6, k.2, m.1, k.1. [122 sts.]
*9th row:* k.4, (p.6, k.6) 9 times, p.6, k.4.
*11th row:* as 9th row.
*13th row:* k.1, m.1, p.6, (k.6, p.6) 4 times, k.12, (p.6, k.6) 4 times, p.6, m.1, k.1. [124 sts.]
*15th row:* p.2, (k.6, p.6) 4(5) times, k.12, (p.6, k.6) 4(5) times, p.2.
*17th row:* as 15th row.
*19th row:* p.1, m.1, p.4, (k.6, p.6) 9 times, k.6, p.4, m.1, p.1. [126 sts.]
*21st row:* p.6, (k.6, p.6) 10 times.
*23rd row:* as 21st row.
*24th row:* k. all k. sts. and p. all p. sts.
These 24 rows set the patt.

All sizes:
Cont. in patt., moving patt. outwards from centre marker by 3 sts. on next and every foll. 6th row.
AT THE SAME TIME, inc. 1 st. at each end of next and every foll. 6th row to obtain 118(132:146) sts.
Cont. straight, but still moving patt. outwards from centre, until back measures 33 cm. (13 in.), ending with a wrong side row.

### Shape Armholes

Keeping patt. correct, cast off 4 sts. at beg. of next 2 rows.
Dec. 1 st. at each end of next 3(5:7) rows.
Work 1 row.
Dec. 1 st. at each end of next and every foll. alt. row until 96(104:112) sts. rem.
Work straight until back measures 53(55:56) cm. (20¾(21½:22) in.), ending with a wrong side row.

### Shape Shoulders

Cast off 9(10:10) sts. at beg. of next 4 rows.
Cast off 9(9:11) sts. at beg. of foll. 2 rows.
Cast off rem. 42(46:50) sts.

## FRONT

Work as back until only 32 rows rem. to start of shoulder shaping, ending with a wrong side row.

### Shape Neck

Keeping patt. correct, divide for neck as folls.:
*Next row:* patt. 46(50:54), work 2 sts. tog., turn and leave rem. sts. on spare needle.
Dec. 1 st. at neck edge on every row until 37 sts. rem.
Work 1 row.
Dec. 1 st. at neck edge on next and every foll. alt. row until 27(29:31) sts. rem.
Work 1 row.

### Shape Shoulder

Work as on back.
Return to sts. on spare needle, rejoin yarn, work 2 sts. tog., patt. to end.
Finish to match 1st side reversing all shapings.

## RIGHT SLEEVE

** Cast on 50(54:58) sts. with 3¼mm. needles.
Work in k.2, p.2, rib as on back, ending with 1st row.
*Next row:* rib 3(5:3), * m.1, rib 5(9:4), rep. from * to last 2(4:3) sts., m.1, rib to end. [60(60:72) sts.]
Change to 4mm. needles and work in patt. as folls.: **
*1st row* (right side): (k.6, p.6) 5(5:6) times.
*2nd and every alt. row:* k. all k. sts. and p. all p. sts.

*3rd and 5th rows:* as 1st row.
*7th row:* p.3, (k.6, p.6) 4(4:5) times, k.6, p.3.
*9th and 11th rows:* as 7th row.
*13th row:* p.1, m.1, p.5, (k.6, p.6) 4(4:5) times, k.5, m.1, k.1.
Cont. in patt., moving patt. 3 sts. to the *left* on every foll. 6th row.
AT THE SAME TIME, inc. 1 st. at each end of every foll. 6th(6th:7th) row to obtain 92(98:104) sts.
Work straight, still moving patt., until sleeve measures 46(47:48) cm. (18½(18½:18¾) in.), ending with a wrong side row.

### Shape Top

Keeping patt. correct, cast off 4 sts. at beg. of next 2 rows.
Dec. 1 st. at each end of next and every foll. alt. row until 50(50:54) sts. rem.
Work 1 row.
Dec. 1 st. at each end of next and every foll. row until only 26 sts. rem.
Cast off.

## LEFT SLEEVE

Work as right sleeve from ** to **.
*1st row* (right side): (p.6, k.6) 5(5:6) times.
*2nd and every alt row:* k. all k. sts. and p. all p. sts.
*3rd and 5th rows:* as 1st row.
*7th row:* p.3, (k.6, p.6) 4(4:5) times, k.6, p.3.
*9th and 11th rows:* as 7th row.
*13th row:* k.1, m.1, k.5, (p.6, k.6) 4(4:5) times, p.5, m.1, k.1.
Cont. in patt., moving patt. 3 sts. to the *right* on every foll. 6th row.
AT THE SAME TIME, inc. for sides to match right sleeve.
Finish to match first sleeve.

## NECKBAND

Cast on 2 sts. with 3¼mm. needles.
Work in garter st. (every row k.).
AT THE SAME TIME, inc. 1 st. at beg. of next and every foll. alt. row to obtain 8 sts.
Cont. as folls.:
*1st row:*
*2nd row:* k.1, m.1, k. to last 2 sts., k.2 tog. (8 sts. left).
Rep. 1st and 2nd rows until shorter side is long enough to fit round neck edge *on top of work,* ending with 1st row.
Dec. 1 st. at beg. of next and every foll. alt. row until 2 sts. rem.
Work 1 row.
K.2 sts. tog. and fasten off.

## MAKING UP

Press every piece following instructions on ball bands.
Sew up shoulder seams.
Sew up side and sleeve seams.
Set in sleeves.
Sew up short slanted ends of neckband, thus forming a point.
Position neckband on top of work and sew up inner edge to neckline edge.
Sew up outer edge of neckline loosely.
Press seams if required.